DATE DUE

MY 1 '64			
DE 18 '64	RESERVE		
MR 4'66	Winter '87		
MY 17'66	Winter '91		
AP 10'70	RESERVE		
AP 28'70	Reserve Winter 92		
JY 17 70	NOV 23 1992		
	NOV 15 1995		
AG 18'70	NOV 20 1995		
Reserve	NOV 13		
Reserve	Reserve Winter '02		
01-06-78	NOV 17 2002		
RESERVE	NOV 01		
NOV 0 3 1982			
RESERVE			
Win 82			
RESERVE			
Winter 85			
0 8 1985			
ORD			PRINTED IN U.S.A.

Prophets in Perspective

Prophets in Perspective

B. D. NAPIER

Abingdon Press   NEW YORK   NASHVILLE

PROPHETS IN PERSPECTIVE

SET UP, PRINTED, AND BOUND BY THE
PARTHENON   PRESS,   AT   NASHVILLE,
TENNESSEE, UNITED STATES OF AMERICA

TO

THE MEMORY OF

Alice Osborne Napier

For thus said the Lord Yahweh, the Holy One of Israel,
  "In returning and rest you shall be saved;
in quietness and confidence shall be your strength."
                                        (ISA. 30:15)

When Israel was a child, I loved him,
  and out of Egypt I called my son.
The more I called them,
  the more they went from me;

.   .   .   .

Yet it was I who taught Ephraim to walk,
  I took them up in my arms;

.   .   .   .

I led them with cords of compassion,
  with the bands of love;

.   .   .   .

  and I bent down to them and fed them.

They shall return to the land of Egypt,

.   .   .   .

  because they have refused to return to me.

How can I give you up, O Ephraim!
  How can I hand you over, O Israel!
My heart recoils within me,
  my compassion grows warm and tender.

.   .   .   .

For I am God and not man, the Holy One in your midst,
  and I will not come to destroy!
                                        (HOS. 11:1-9)

It is too light a thing that you should be my servant
   to raise up the tribes of Jacob
   and to restore the preserved of Israel;
I will give you as a light to the nations,
   that my salvation may reach to the end of the earth.

                                (Isa. 49:6)

My Word shall not return to me empty,
   but it shall accomplish that which I purpose,
   and prosper in the thing for which I sent it.

                               (Isa. 55:11)

Preface

THE STORY IS TOLD OF A LITTLE GIRL WHO APPROACHED HER librarian one day and asked for a book on penguins. The book was found, and she went eagerly home with it. The next morning she was waiting to return the book when the library opened. "I wanted to learn something about penguins," she said sadly, "but not this much."

Prophets in Perspective first began to take shape a few years ago when I was asked to write an almost book-length article on "Prophet and Prophetism" for *The Interpreter's Dictionary of the Bible*. Before the article was finally submitted it underwent the critical scrutiny of one of my seminars at the Yale University Divinity School. The article appeared with the publication of the IDB in the fall of 1962.

After considerable alteration and revision, parts of that study of prophetism were delivered in February, 1961, as the Jackson Lectures at Perkins School of Theology in Dallas. I welcome this opportunity to thank Abingdon Press for permission to use the material, and to express my appreciation to all who helped make that occasion such a memorable one for me, and for Mrs. Napier, who accompanied me.

The subject matter of the article and lectures was the basis of a three-weeks' course of study at the Eastern Pastors' School of the (now) United Church of Christ, at Deering, New Hampshire, in the summer of 1961. Sections of the Lectures have also been delivered before college groups and church lay people.

Now, for this small volume, my study of prophetism has been renewed, further revised, and expanded.

I suppose one can get more than one wants of penguins or prophets. This book was not written with the little girl in mind. Graduate theological students have found some sections to be ground-breaking exploration for them. At the same time, however, lay people, college students, and parish ministers have given attentive and comprehending hearing to this discussion of prophetism. They have made constructive suggestions which have been gratefully incorporated, and they have persistently urged its publication in this form.

I have not tried to write a breezy popularization of Old Testament prophetism, but a serious, responsible, comprehensive review of that phenomenal movement which produced such giants in the history of religion as Amos, Hosea, Isaiah, Jeremiah, and that crowning figure of prophetism, the Second Isaiah. It is all right for a little girl to learn a little about penguins, but superficial knowledge of religion and theology among adults is rampant and destructive on the American scene, and even within the American church, not entirely excepting, alas, the clergy. Such superficiality needs no further feeding.

I would like to think I have hit a happy medium here, but I would rather the book be returned or discarded than that it satisfy any reader who hopes only to be entertained for an evening by that living prophetism which proclaimed and still proclaims God's judgment and redemption of Israel, and through her life, of the world.   B. D. NAPIER

Contents

Introduction:
Prophetism and Prophet

BROADLY DEFINED, BIBLICAL PROPHETISM BEGINS WITH MOSES and continues without critical interruption in a distinguished succession of persons through both Testaments of the Bible. This prophetism in the broad sense is simply a particular way of looking at history: The *meaning* of history is to be found only in terms of God's concern, purpose, and even participation in history. In this broad definition of prophetism, then, the whole Bible is "prophetic" since it consistently reflects this passionately theological understanding of history.

The very arrangement of the biblical books in the Hebrew canon of scripture presupposes this definition of prophetism.[1] Between the first division of the Law and the third division of the Writings, the central category of the Prophets embraces not only the books of the prophets Isaiah, Jeremiah, Ezekiel, and the twelve prophets from Hosea to Malachi (all together termed "Latter Prophets") but also the historical writings of Joshua, Judges, and the books of Samuel and Kings ("Former Prophets"). In this way the Hebrew Bible formally and appropriately acknowledges that prophetism is more than the prophet and his work, that it is also a way of looking at, understanding, and interpreting history.

More narrowly defined, of course, prophetism is the function of a particular succession of men—notably, Amos, Hosea, Isaiah, Micah, Jeremiah, Ezekiel, and the Second Isaiah. These prophets all appear within the span of about two centuries, between, roughly, the middle of the eighth and the middle of the sixth centuries. They are preceded and even anticipated, however, by a Nathan in the tenth century and an Elijah in the ninth, and they are followed by a succession of distinguished but lesser lights in the sixth and fifth centuries.

The influence of this prophetism of the prophets on the biblical record itself is overwhelming. No significant segment of biblical literature has come down to us unmodified by that prophetic epoch.[2]

The Terms in the Bible

The Hebrew word for prophet is a common noun appearing more than three hundred times in the Old Testament. It is applied to a remarkable range of characters appearing from Gen. 20:7 to Mal. 4:5, and to surprisingly disparate personalities from Aaron (Exod. 7:1) to Elijah (I Kings 17-19, 21), from the "true" to the "false" (e.g., I Kings 22), from the relatively primitive (e.g., I Sam. 10) to the relatively sophisticated (the Isaiahs, for example), from the highly visionary (see Ezek. 1-2) to the concretely ethical (Amos, or Nathan in II Sam. 12, or Elijah in I Kings 21), from the seemingly objective perspective (of Amos, for example) to the intensely participating attitude (of Jeremiah). This is only to suggest the breadth of range of application of the term in the Old Testament.[3]

In the New Testament the term appears commonly in

14

reference to the prophets of the Old, and predominantly in Matthew and Luke-Acts. Both Jesus (Matt. 21:11; cf. Matt. 13:57, Mark 6:4, and Luke 4:24) and John the Baptist (Matt. 11:7 ff. and parallels) are regarded as prophets. Paul understands that the essential prophetic function continues in the life of the church (see I Cor. 12 and 14). Judas and Silas, for example, are subsequently interpreted in that role (Acts 15:32); while the early Christian community at Antioch knows the presence of "prophets and teachers" (Acts 13:1). Like the Old Testament prophet, the New Testament prophet conveys the divinely imparted meaning of history (cf. Acts 21:10), but signs of degeneration are suggested in Paul's implicit condemnation of extreme manifestations of prophecy in I Cor. 13. It would appear that the role of prophet in the New Testament sometimes assumed the same extreme ecstatic form that appears also in the Old.

Prophet in Biblical Hebrew

The Hebrew term for prophet, the only term appropriately so translated, is *nabi'*. I Sam. 9:9 recalls the fact that "he who is now called a prophet (*nabi'*) was formerly called a seer (*ro'eh*)." The Greek translation of this verse in the Septuagint [4] presupposes a slightly different text, conveying the sense that the term "seer" was in the past simply a common, popular name for prophet. The fact remains that one term only is normative in the Old Testament. What does that term, *nabi'*, mean? Unfortunately, we do not know and cannot now determine the original meaning of the root. Two verb forms frequently appear (*pi'el* and *hitpa'el*), unquestionably derived from the noun, but they simply mean "to

15

play the *nabi'* role"; that is, "to act the *nabi'* part." It is a good guess, but only a guess, that the lost Hebrew root is related to cognate Accadian and Arabic words meaning "to call" or "to announce." The underlying meaning of the Hebrew noun might be, then, "an announcer," or "the one who announces" the purpose and activity of God. Or, is the passive sense primary? Is the prophet the recipient of the announcement of God; is he then one who is called?

Even if we were certain of the original meaning of the root underlying the Hebrew noun we could hardly take this as conclusive evidence of the basic understanding of the Old Testament prophet in the middle centuries of the first millenium B.C. Rather, we will have to understand the sense of the term *nabi'* from the person of the prophet himself as he appears and functions in the community of ancient Israel.

NOTES

[1] See *The Interpreter's Bible* (Nashville: Abingdon Press, 1952), I, 32 ff.

[2] So Gerhard von Rad, *Theologie des Alten Testaments* (Munich, 1957), I, 76.

[3] For another kind of survey of prophetic variety, see H. H. Rowley, *The Servant of the Lord* (London: Lutterworth Press, 1952), pp. 102 ff.

[4] The Hebrew scriptures were translated into Greek beginning in the third century, B.C.

I
Prophet and Prophets

WHAT IS TO BE SAID OF THE PROPHET AS HE APPEARS AS PERSON, even professional person, in the life and times of ancient Israel? What are his significant connections, associations, relationships, within the institutional complexes of Israelite society? What are for us the most instructive, if debated, areas in the prophets' relationships?

The Seer

The Hebrew terms *ḥozeh* and *ro'eh* are both properly translated "seer." Both terms appear in contexts suggesting some parallel in function with the prophet. Outside Chronicles which is relatively late and where, in any case, no significant occurrence of the terms appears, the term *ḥozeh* appears six times and *ro'eh* seven. It is *ḥozeh* in II Sam. 24:11 (of uncertain date, but not conventionally assigned to the "A" or early source in Samuel) where "the prophet Gad" is "David's seer." In II Kings 17:13 prophet and seer are together to warn Israel and Judah. In Isa. 29:10 the characteristic Hebrew poetic parallelism of members puts prophet and seer again in the same essential function:

> For the Lord has poured out upon you
> a spirit of deep sleep,

and has closed your eyes, the prophets,
and covered your heads, the seers.

In the same way, Mic. 3:7 couples seers and diviners (from a
root *qsm*).

The seers shall be disgraced
and the diviners put to shame.

The fifth occurrence of *ḥozeh* is in Amos 7:12, in the narrative of Amos' encounter with Amaziah, the priest of Bethel.
Here, too, the effect is a near-equating of seer and prophet:
"And Amaziah said to Amos, 'O seer, go, flee away to the
land of Judah, and eat bread there, and *prophesy* there. . . .' "
The verb "prophesy" is the common denominative form
(probably from *nabi'*). Clearly, it is the appropriate function
of the seer to act the part of the prophet. Whatever else is
involved in Amos' response in vs. 14, he means to repudiate
Amaziah's implicit charge of professionalism, the strong insinuation that Amos has mouthed merely the "party line"
of the seers and prophets.

In all these occurrences of *ḥozeh,* with the single exception of Mic. 3:7, seer and prophet are, to all intents and
purposes, indistinguishable.

The second term for seer, *ro'eh* appears in Isa. 30:10 in
parallelism with the first, *ḥozeh.* Here is a literal translation
of the verse, in which the two terms are equated.

18

"For they are a rebellious people . . ." (vs. 9) :
  who say to the seers *(ro'eh,* plural) ,
  "See not"
  and to the seers *(ḥozeh,* plural) ,
  "See not for us
  that which is right;
  speak to us smooth things,
  see illusions!"

If there ever existed any real distinction between the two terms for seer, it is nowhere apparent in the Old Testament.

If, now, we recall again the statement of I Sam. 9:9 that "he who is now called a prophet [*nabi'*] was formerly called a seer [*ro'eh*]" we must conclude that prophet and seer were understood as exercising in common the function of *seeing*— i.e., apprehending that which is not in the normal course accessible—and *speaking* forth, proclaiming, that which is thus seen and apprehended. The R.S.V. properly renders Isa. 30:10 not in literal translation but in sympathetic and accurate interpretation:

> For they are a rebellious people . . .
> . . . .
> who say to the seers, "See not";
>   and to the prophets, "Prophesy not to us what is
>   right;
> speak to us smooth things,
>   prophesy illusions. . . ."

The seer-prophet apprehends not necessarily that which is

19

smooth, but emphatically that which is right. His function, prophetism, is never reception alone, but reception-articulation: To see is to prophesy!

The designation of Samuel as seer in the old narrative of I Sam. 9^1 and the parenthetical statement of 9:9—inserted later into the account—that the seer becomes in time the prophet make it clear that the office of seer existed among Israelites before that of prophet. The biblical evidence we have just surveyed points to a period of coexistence of seer and prophet and a popular tendency to equate the two offices. Israelite prophetism, which began to emerge as an institution in the tenth century, is indebted to the office of seer, but also, as we are about to see, to the very different phenomenon of ancient Canaanite prophetism, long current in the land when Israel entered and settled there.

Mature Israelite prophetism was an appropriation, then, transacted on the ground of Canaan over a period of several centuries. Its unique character, however, was shaped neither by seer nor by Canaanite prophet, but by the nature of Yahwism and the Yahweh faith. This is to affirm that, while the institution of Israelite prophetism developed relatively slowly and attained maturity relatively late, the essence of the prophetic was present from the Mosaic era, inherent in the faith of ancient Israel from her formation as a people out of Egyptian slavery.

Old Testament prophetism in its development from the tenth to the sixth centuries represents a striking refinement and transformation of both the office of seer and the institution of Canaanite prophetism.

The Contagious Prophet

Classical Israelite prophetism is related to and influenced by the seer. It is also indebted to a kind of prophetic role and person at home in Canaan long before Israel and from early times identified by the term *nabi'*, prophet. This prophetism in its Canaanite expression first appears in the Old Testament in the old narrative of I Sam. 9:1–10:16. In the hope of locating his father's lost asses, Saul and his servant have consulted the seer, Samuel, who has not only reassured them on the score of the animals but has also anointed Saul "to be prince over his people Israel" (10:1). As sign and token of the validity of Samuel's act Saul is informed in advance of what is to take place, and it happens precisely as Samuel has said it would:

When they came to Gibeah, behold, a band of prophets met him; and the spirit of God came mightily upon him, and he prophesied among them. And when all who knew him before saw how he prophesied with the prophets, the people said to one another, "What has come over the son of Kish? Is Saul also among the prophets?" . . . Therefore it became a proverb, "Is Saul also among the prophets?" (10:10-12.)

I Sam. 19:18-24 repeats the proverb in a more dramatic setting, with marked emphasis upon the highly contagious nature of the seizure and an elaboration of its manifestation. Saul, in pursuit of the now outlawed David, who has taken refuge with Samuel, sends a company of men to capture David. "And when they saw the company of the prophets prophesying, and Samuel standing as head over them, the Spirit of God came upon the messengers of Saul, and they

21

also prophesied." (19:20.) Two subsequent companies are dispatched, and both remain, seized by the same contagion. Now Saul comes: "And the Spirit of God came upon him also, and as he went he prophesied until he came to Naioth in Ramah. And he too stripped off his clothes, And he too prophesied before Samuel, and lay naked all that day and all that night. Hence it is said, 'Is Saul also among the prophets?' " (19:23-24.)

The relationship between the narrative of I Sam. 10 and that of chapter 19 is uncertain. Source critics have commonly seen the second as a duplicate account, a later and therefore allegedly unauthentic explanation of the proverb. For our purpose here, this question is irrelevant. Both passages may be taken, regardless of relationship and date, as valid commentary on the phenomenon of Canaanite prophetism.

This prophetism is patently a totally different office from that of the seer. Not now, certainly not yet, could one equate seer and prophet. If, as an actual item of pragmatic history, Samuel functioned both as seer (I Sam. 9) and ecstatic prophet (I Sam. 19), the roles remained separate—they were in no sense interdependent. Seer and prophet are as yet of very different stuff. The seer appears as an office long familiar and thoroughly at home among Israelites, quite conceivably dating from pre-Canaan times, but this earliest reference to contagious prophecy conveys the atmosphere of the alien. Israel is not at home with it, and an unmistakable Israelite, this son of Kish, graces it strangely indeed: "Is Saul also among the prophets?" This institution has not yet been appropriated by Israelites, or, if in process of appropriation, it has not yet been domiciled and certainly not yet integrated into the pattern of familiar Israelite existence.

What, here, is the content of the noun "prophet" and the verb "prophesy"? Observe first that the phenomenon of prophecy is induced: Samuel says to Saul, "You will meet a band of prophets coming down from the high place with harp, tambourine, flute, and lyre before them, prophesying" (I Sam. 10:5). The ecstatic emotional state is at least in part produced and maintained by the use of music. Observe further that a total transformation in personality occurs: "You shall prophesy with them and be turned into another man" (vs. 6). Again, this state of prophesying is created and sustained as a group phenomenon. It can, further, be spread by contagion; it can be "caught." It is popularly interpreted as seizure by the deity, in which regard the prevailing, but not exclusive (10:6 reads "Spirit of Yahweh"), divine name employed is the weak and colorless *'elohim*. This is in any case a different kind of seizure from the *charisma,* the more or less permanent "endowment" of a chosen person by the Spirit of Yahweh (e.g., I Sam. 16:13 ff.), a phenomenon which belongs centrally to Israel and Yahwism.

The brilliant description of the frantic performance of the prophets of Baal on Mount Carmel in I Kings 18 gives further definition to the phenomenon of contagious, ecstatic prophecy. The contest between the prophets of Baal and the prophet of Yahweh (Elijah) is under way, and Baal's prophets have induced the seizure and are sustaining it in an effort to evoke a tangible response from their deity. Crying "O Baal, answer us!" they perform a kind of limping dance, and as Elijah taunts them, their wild performance reaches its emotionally uncontrolled peak when they "cut themselves *after their custom* with swords and lances until the blood gushed out upon them" (I Kings 18:28). Noon, Baal's best and strongest hour, passes, but the prophets of Baal—note the language of the text—"continue to prophesy" (vs. 29). The R.S.V. is forced to interpret: "they raved on." "The verb [from the same root as *nabi*', "prophet"] can only be paraphrased in Christian language, which confines 'prophecy' to the higher levels of revelation." [3] But precisely so we are eloquently informed on the content of this original, alien, Canaanite phenomenon of prophet and prophetism. This is the prophet. This is his prophecy. This is to prophesy!

Now, if this is a far remove from the content of "seer" and "seeing," it is at least an equally far remove from the prophet and the prophetism exemplified even in Ezekiel, to say nothing of Isaiah! Whatever may be the ultimate judgment with respect to the factor of "ecstasy" in the great prophets of Israel, it cannot legitimately be argued that their prophetism is in continuum with and perpetuates this phenomenon of Canaanite prophecy. Where is any significant biblical evidence that classical Israelite prophetism was predominantly manifested in a temporary and artificially induced state; that it was productive of a totally transformed personality; that it was a group-created-and-sustained state of emotion and, as such, a highly contagious condition induced by violent seizure and involving the absolute suspension of rationality?

It has, of course, occasionally been so argued.[4] The interpretation of Old Testament prophetism as an essentially ecstatic phenomenon differing not at all in this respect from the ecstatic prophecy characteristic of the ancient Near and

24

Middle East continues to be advocated, especially by those who are persuaded of prevailing ancient Eastern institutional uniformity.[5]

It would be out of place here to discuss the scope and variation in interpretation of the relationship between the great prophets and the phenomenon of contagious prophecy. I can see no evidence justifying the claim that the two are essentially identical. If the term "ecstasy" is applied at all to the giant figures in the succession from Amos to Second Isaiah, I would want to insist on Lindblom's distinction between ecstasy of the absorption type (involving loss of rational control) and that of the concentration type, and a very clear further distinction between the circumspective religion of the prophets and the more common ancient Eastern type of introspective, mystical piety. *Unio mystica,* that state in which the mystic is absorbed into union with the deity, is quite alien to Israel. The ecstatic element in classical prophetism, insofar as it exists at all, is largely confined to the prophets' profound concentration, which may result in the suspension of normal consciousness and the total, if brief, interruption of normal sense perception.[6]

The Role of Form Criticism

Form-critical studies in the prophets have thrown considerable light on the question of the ecstatic factor in prophetism. The analysis of a characteristic prophetic form of utterance (German: *Gattung*) defines both the subject of "ecstatic" concentration and at the same time the nature and significance of the unmistakably non-ecstatic; that is, the role of the prophet's normally functioning senses. Form criticism points out a characteristic prophetic utterance in two intimately related parts. The first is the speech of invective (German: *Scheltrede*), often extended and eloquent, commonly passionate and bitter, and always portraying, although in different ways, the mind of the prophet, the *man* the prophet. The second part, immediately following, is the word of judgment (German: *Drohwort*. "Threat" is not quite adequate; perhaps "contingent judgment"). This is brief, pointed, powerful, devastating, sometimes terrifyingly impersonal, and characteristically devoid of personal-human animus. These repeatedly conjoined parts, the prophet's free invective as extended prelude to the fearfully compact pronouncement of divine judgment, constitute a basic pattern of prophetic speech.

As an illustration consider Isaiah's familiar prophetic outburst that begins, "Ho, Assyria, rod of my wrath!" in 10:5 ff. The invective is here remarkably extended and continues with eloquent vigor through vs. 15. All this is the prophet's own utterance, and it would be absurd to contend that this (vss. 5-15) is the product of a supranormal psychological experience, the articulation of ecstatic reception. Here one witnesses a deftly balanced interplay of intellect and emotion, and these not merely controlled, but highly disciplined, responsive, obedient. The range in verbal mode testifies both to the vast breadth of prophetic sensitivities and the high order of prophetic intelligence. Here one is confronted by responses at once brilliant and intuitive from a succession of perspectives: Yahweh, Initiating Covenanter with David-Zion-Judah (vss. 5-6); an astute political observer who does not question the Lordship of Yahweh in history (vs. 7); a personified Assyria, with artful dramatic identification (vss. 8-11); the same faith-political position of vs. 7 enunciated again, now in castigation of pride (vs. 12; this is a central theme of Isaiah); Assyria again, characterized in her own words and prophetically condemned in highly deft verbal form:

> My hand has found like a nest
> the wealth of the peoples . . .
> And there was none that moved a wing
> or opened the mouth, or chirped. (See vss. 13-14.)

So to a conclusion in the full power of the prophet's own devastating sarcasm:

> Shall the ax vaunt itself over him who hews with it,
> or the saw magnify itself against him who wields it? (Vs. 15.)

By what possible definition of ecstasy can the skillfully combined elements of articulation in this speech be explained?

This is not to say that ecstasy in the sense of supranormal concentration plays no role. All this, in now conventional form-critical analysis, is a part of, a prelude to, and called forth by, the word of judgment, the *Drohwort* (vs. 16), which may very well have come to the prophet in ecstasy, in ecstatic concentration. The prophet's own extended speech of invective (vss. 5-15) represents his considered application, timing, and interpretation of the Word of Yahweh (the *Drohwort,* vs. 16) which he *hears, sees,* or, involving all the

27

senses directed totally inward, *perceives.* Psychologically, of course, this is the most important part of the prophetic utterance.

In the relationship between these two primary and inseparable parts of prophetic preaching the controversy over the role and nature of ecstasy is resolved. The prophet receives the actual *dabar,* the real Word of Yahweh, in ecstatic concentration. This is a primary form of the biblical phenomenon of revelation. The Word thus received is not always precisely intelligible, however, in a process of recall which requires its appropriation in the rational mode. The prophet, in consequence, feels himself called upon by means of the speech of invective to interpret and direct, to point and apply the word of judgment, the revealed Word of Yahweh. This he does, in most glaring contrast with the ecstatic state of the Word's reception, in a process of deliberation. The compact and, certainly on occasion, enigmatic divine Word is mulled over, reflected upon, wrestled with. This process, which involves the full range of the prophet's best rational powers, becomes his prophetic work, his ministerial task, his professional exercise. It is his prophetic obligation to determine how, in what context, when and to whom, and in what way most effectively this word of judgment is to be delivered. To this end he composes the speech of invective and places it immediately before the received word, characteristically marking the transition with some such particle as "therefore" (*laken*) :

> *Therefore,* the Lord, Yahweh of hosts
> will send wasting sickness
> among his stout warriors,

and under his glory a burning will
be kindled like the burning of fire. (Isa. 10:16.)

The conventional literary-critical judgment that the following verses (17-19) were not part of the original unit is doubtless correct, but the standard critical conclusions on vs. 16—fragmentary, a corrupt text, distorted in transmission, et cetera—result from the failure to recognize the difference in form and the functional relationship between *Scheltrede* and *Drohwort,* the deliberated and composed invective called forth by the received Word, the divine threat or judgment.

This smaller unit (vs. 16) toward which the whole passage is pointed [7] is the reproduction—insofar as such is capable of reproduction—of the word received in prophetic concentration/ecstasy. It differs radically in verbal temperament from the speech of invective. What is perceived (is it heard or seen, or must we say simply that it is sensed?) is a wasting sickness among warriors and a burning fire beneath a prideful magnificence. Whose warriors? Whose pride? Why is this so? How, when, and to what purpose shall it be proclaimed? If the wasting and the burning, the sickness and the fire, are undefined certainties out of ecstasy, it is the prophet's hard task by sweat and tears to define the symbols of vision/audition and to determine and declare their meaning. This is not to exclude inspiration and revelation from the task, but this part of the prophetic function, the speech of invective, certainly does not have its origin in any kind of ecstasy.

The prophet no doubt underwent what not only we but also his own generation would see as outside the limits of normal experience. Perhaps in none of the great prophets was there a total absence of the supranormal psychological manifestation; but both form and content of Israelite prophetism stand in restraint of persistent tendencies to overstress the ecstatic element in the prophet.

The Institutional Prophet

There is no doubt that associations of prophets existed in ancient Israel. Groups or guilds of prophets are attested over the whole range of the history of the kingdoms from the time of Saul in the eleventh century B.C. until the fall of Jerusalem in the early sixth century B.C. Nor is there any question that these associated professional prophets were related to the cultus and/or the court and regularly discharged certain cultic professional duties. Functionaries known as prophets were cultically institutionalized precisely as were the priests and other sanctuary personnel. It appears certain that such prophets were attached to the temple in Jerusalem and that some time before the work of the Chronicler (Ezra-Nehemiah, I and II Chronicles in the fourth or third century B.C.) the temple prophets became temple singers and merged with the other Levitical orders.[8]

The function of prophetism as institutionalized at sanctuary or court is not in question. The real question has to do with the extent of this association and the possibility that we actually have traces in the canonical Old Testament of the work of such institutional prophets. The real question has further to do with the possibility that the great prophets of the Old Testament lived out their careers in such associations and were in fact themselves such associated cult functionaries. This aspect of the question of the relationship of the great prophets to cult prophetism remains complex and thoroughly vexed. We must reject extreme positions which seek to clarify all possible uncertainties in Old Testament prophetism by analogy with associations of cultic personnel in ancient Mesopotamia, the broader West Semitic areas, and in Arabia. This basic assumption of a uniform religious phenomenology over the ancient East leads ultimately to the conclusion that the great prophets, without exception, are to be interpreted essentially and dominantly in terms of the common category of cult personnel. Not only Jeremiah and Ezekiel—whose possible official relationship to the temple has long been recognized in the fact that both were priests before they were prophets—but also Amos and Isaiah, are in this extreme position alleged to show complete identity with earlier cult prophets.[9]

It is in order now to look again at Amos 7:14 and to repeat in the present discussion a comment already made with reference to contagious prophecy: "Then Amos answered Amaziah, 'I am no prophet, nor a prophet's son; but I am a herdsman, and a dresser of sycamore trees.'" In denying that he is—or "was"—a prophet, it is possible that Amos means to reject any insinuation that he is himself an ecstatic prophet or a professional cult prophet, and at the same time, to dissociate himself from and repudiate the cult prophetism at the Bethel sanctuary, over which Amaziah presided.

The cultic-institutional interpretation of the great prophets has been greatly in vogue in the past few decades. The attempt to fit biblical prophetism into this category has been stimulated not only by studies of cult festivals all over the ancient Near East, but also by the alleged reconstruction of Israel's celebration of the New Year and the Enthronement

31

Day of the sacral king—that is, the king in the role of Yahweh. This is claimed to have been achieved by the application of the principle of environmental analogy and by form-critical analysis of certain Old Testament texts, especially in the Psalms. Even the account of the call of the prophet Isaiah (Isa. 6) has been analyzed in such a way as to make of the prophet a cult functionary whose call experience can be understood only in the terms and images of the annual festival of the enthronement of the sacral king centering in the Jerusalem temple. In this view a basic cultic mode of thought, common to the ancient Middle Eastern culture, is seen. Isaiah becomes one with the cult prophet, his words reflecting living cultic conditions, the core of which is the institution of sacral kingship.[10]

The mass of alleged evidence in support of such identity is at first glance, impressive, but its structure, upon examination, appears at points to be insubstantial. Simpler interpretations of Isaiah's call are more natural.[11] Further reservations appear when we look closely at another item of support for the thesis that the great prophets were merely cult prophets.

It has been proposed from the statement in Jer. 29:26 that the associations of *kohanim* (priests) and *nebi'im* (prophets) were organized under a common leader entitled *kohen,* and the conclusion is drawn that the classical *nabi'* too was a cult functionary. It is also assumed that Jeremiah must be identified simply as one of the associated cult prophets.[12]

The passage in question immediately follows an extended letter from Jeremiah (29:1-23) to persons exiled from Jerusalem in 597 B.C., a decade before the fall of the city. Jer.

29:26 ff. purports to be the words of one Shemaiah, prominent among the exiles in Babylonia, addressed chiefly to Zephaniah, the senior priest in charge of the temple priests in Jerusalem:

Yahweh has made you priest . . . to have charge in the house of Yahweh over every madman who prophesies, to put him in stocks and collar. Now why have you not rebuked Jeremiah of Anathoth who is prophesying to you? For he has sent to us in Babylon saying, "Your exile will be long; build houses and live in them, and plant gardens and eat their produce." Zephaniah the priest read this letter in the hearing of Jeremiah the prophet. Then the word of Yahweh came to Jeremiah. . . . (29:26-30.)

This has been seriously submitted as weighty evidence that Jeremiah was one of the prophesying attendants on the cultus. But the passage does not even necessarily confirm the cultic institution of prophetism, to say nothing of Jeremiah's integral relationship thereto! On the contrary, this passage appears to be designed as a repudiation of identity between Jeremiah and any prophesying madmen, whether occasional ecstatic orators in the temple area or attached personnel. The powerful import of the passage, executed in devastating rebuke and at the expense of Shemaiah, is precisely to stress the polarity between "prophesying" prophets and *the* prophet, between madness and "the Word of Yahweh."

We must reject, then, the view equating and identifying Yahwistic prophetism, as exemplified in the classical prophets with that widespread prophetism of the cultic association. A line of crucial distinction between the two appears in a study of late eighteenth-century B.C. texts from Mari on the

Upper Euphrates, in which prophetlike persons appear a thousand years before the canonical Old Testament prophets. Here, even if we assume some historical connection between the messenger of God in the Mari texts and the prophet of the Old Testament, we are struck by the radical difference in the character and content of the divine message which the prophet receives. At Mari the divine word deals with cult and political matters of very limited importance. But biblical prophetism proclaims that the great contemporary events in the world are part of a process willed and in outcome determined by God. In sharpest contrast to the prophetic phenomenon at Mari, the great prophets always speak in the name of Yahweh whose will all powers of history serve and whose Word impinges decisively upon all existence.[13]

The profound contrast between the great prophet and the cult prophet is in the *content* of prophetism. I do not mean to preclude the possibility of affiliation of some of the great prophets with cultic associations of prophets, much less the existence of such associations. If there were such affiliation, however, it would be wrong to assess and evaluate any of the "name" Yahweh prophets of the Old Testament in terms of simple identity with the conventional cult prophet.

NOTES

[1] I Sam. 9 is almost unanimously assigned by source critics to the "A" or early source in Samuel.

[2] The Hebrew term for God was YHWH, probably pronounced Yahweh, although this is difficult to know since the language was originally written without vowels.

[3] James A. Montgomery, "The Books of Kings," *International Critical Commentary* (New York: Charles Scribner's Sons, 1952), p. 303.

[4] G. Hölscher first brought this argument to prominence in *Die Profeten* (Leipzig, 1914).

[5] See A. Haldar, *Associations of Cult Prophets Among the Ancient Semites* (Uppsala, 1945).

[6] See further J. Lindblom, "Grundfragen der alttestamentlichen Wissenschaft," *Festschrift Alfred Bertholet* (Tübingen, 1950), pp. 325 ff. Here Lindblom quotes with strong approval Harold Knight, *The Hebrew Prophetic Consciousness* (London: Lutterworth Press, 1948), p. 96: "Here we have a state of the highest integration, for the attention is wholly focused upon a single object which gradually fills the consciousness until the connexion between the subject and the outside world is broken."

[7] See *The Interpreter's Bible*, 5, 240.

[8] Aubrey R. Johnson, *The Cultic Prophet in Ancient Israel* (Cardiff, Wales: University of Wales Press, 1944), p. 60. See also Sigmund Mowinckel, *Psalmenstudien, III: Die Kultprophetie und prophetische Psalmen* (Kristiania, 1923). Cf. Haldar, *op. cit.;* but see also H. H. Rowley "Ritual and the Hebrew Prophets," *Journal of Semitic Studies* (1956), pp. 338 ff.

[9] So Haldar, *op. cit.,* especially pp. 111-21.

[10] So I. Engnell, *The Call of Isaiah* (Uppsala, 1949), pp. 43 ff. Cf. the excellent, and more moderate, study by Aubrey R. Johnson, *Sacral Kingship in Ancient Israel* (Cardiff, Wales: University of Wales Press, 1956).

[11] See O. Eissfeldt, "The Prophetic Literature," *The Old Testament and Modern Study,* edited by H. H. Rowley (New York: Oxford University Press, 1951), pp. 125 ff.

[12] Haldar, *op. cit.,* p. 111.

[13] This is according to the thought and sometimes even the language of M. Noth, "History and the Word of God in the Old Testament," *Bulletin of the John Rylands Library,* Vol. 32, No. 2 (March, 1950), pp. 200 ff.

II

Prophet, Cult, and Record

Prophet and Cultus

SCHOLARSHIP OF A PRECEDING GENERATION COMMONLY CHAR-
acterized classical Old Testament prophetism as strongly
anti-cultic. In support of this interpretation passages from
Amos and Isaiah have frequently been cited:

> I hate, I repudiate [R.S.V., "despise"] your feasts,
>   and I take no delight in your solemn assemblies,
> Even though you offer me your burnt offerings and cereal
>   offerings,
>   I will not accept them;
> and the peace offerings of your fatted beasts
>   will I ignore [R.S.V., "I will not look upon"].
> Take away from me the noise of your songs;
>   to the melody of your harps I will not listen.
> But let justice roll along [R.S.V., "roll down"] like waters
> and righteousness like an everflowing stream. (Amos 5:21-
>   24.)

> What to me is the multitude of your sacrifices?
>   says Yahweh:
> I have had enough of burnt offerings of rams
>   and the fat of fed beasts;
> I do not delight in the blood of bulls,

or of lambs, or of he-goats.
When you come to appear before me,
who requires of you this trampling of my courts? (Isa. 1:11-12.)

Your new moons and your appointed feasts
my soul hates. . . .
When you spread forth your hands,
I will hide my eyes from you. . . .
Wash yourselves; make yourselves clean;
remove the evil of your doings from before my eyes;
Cease to do evil,
learn to do good. . . . (Isa. 1:14-17.)

Such lines as these have been taken as signifying the un-qualified prophetic repudiation of the institutionalized ex-pression of religion in Israel, as indicating the positive con-cern of Amos and Isaiah, and indeed of all the great proph-ets, to cut out as a vile malignancy the totality of Israel's cultus. For some interpreters the prophets became the giant protagonists of the Ethical and the brilliant antagonists of any and all institutional religion. In misconceived enthu-siasm, the prophets were not only de-institutionalized, but de-theologized as well. They were defined as lonely geniuses of social reform, while Yahweh the God of the prophets was reduced to the status of benign, amorphous Ethical Incentive.

In more recent years scholarly convention has changed. The ethical culturalists, the anti-institutionalists, the pro-neighbor-anti-God, pro-religion-anti-cult voices, are finding other more fitting champions than the prophets. The now prevailing critical eye looks in broader perspective at the whole structure of Israel's life and history. The prophet's

37

expressed impatience with or even intolerance of the cultus is seen now as castigation not of cult qua cult, not of cultic practice per se, but of the cultus in its present guise. The prophet tilts against the enthusiastic performance and perpetuation of formalized, regularized, prescribed outward acts of piety *when these are unsupported* by qualities of justice and righteousness. The prophet knows no abstraction of justice and righteousness. These are qualities of Yahweh revealed as at once the character and demand of the very God upon whom the whole cultus centers.

A key to the understanding of the prophetic indictment of the cultus is Isa. 1:13, which was deliberately omitted in the longer quotation from Isaiah above:

> Bring no more vain offerings;
> incense is an abomination to me.
> New moon and sabbath and the calling of assemblies—
> I cannot endure iniquity *and* solemn assembly;

The fault lies not in the form itself. The form of religious observance, which is the cultus, becomes heinous when it is perpetuated in an existence whose total structure flatly contradicts that which is symbolized in the form!

In the broad perspective of the history of Israel and the role of prophetism it is hardly possible now to maintain an anti-cult and therefore anti-institutional prophetism in Israel. The cult was from the beginning the tangible expression of the faith of Israel. From the beginning Israel could be Israel only cultically. Israel's understanding of her own divine creation in the exodus event was very early culticized in the

Passover. She interpreted her prehistory, as seen in the persons of the patriarchs, in cultic form, and she continued to appropriate that prehistory cultically in the institution of circumcision. In Israel's understanding of the David-Zion covenant it was essential to celebrate and renew the meaning of this covenant in the great autumnal festival of New Year and Enthronement in the temple in Jerusalem. The cultus embodied the faith of Israel; it was the rehearsal of God's mighty deeds—and therefore, his self-disclosures—of the past; it was, as appropriation of the past, at once also the dramatic conveyance of meaning in the present; and bringing past and present into the immediate continuum of identity, it appropriated in anticipation the future of the people of God and the history of God.[1]

The cult of the contemporary Christian church is no doubt as justifiably castigated as that of ancient Israel. As Christmas and Easter are commonly celebrated by perhaps the majority of celebrants, any latter-day "prophet" might be constrained to cry out, "Thus says the Lord, 'I hate, I repudiate your feasts. . . .'" It is perfectly clear, however, that the articulation and, indeed, the very preservation of Christian faith requires the cultic enactment of birth and death and resurrection—this appropriation of the past for the present and the consequent faithful union of time in hope and confidence in the future.

Yahwistic prophetism remained in close rapport with the cultus. The relationship, indeed, was one of mutual indebtedness. It is obvious that the prophets were familiar with the ritual and meaning of the cultus, that they sometimes spoke in language borrowed from it, that they even quoted directly

39

from its prayers and liturgies, and that the role and meaning of the cultus was itself in turn influenced by prophetic interpretation.

This is not to say that the great prophet was a "cult" or "guild" prophet, a member of an "association" of cult prophets officially and professionally related to the cultic institution in manner and degree comparable to the priest. It is to insist, however, that prophet and priest were not so positively, consistently, and inimically opposed as has sometimes been assumed. The two figures most highly ranked in the traditions of Judaism, Moses and Elijah, are remembered and recorded in the dual role of prophet-priest (Moses is a Levite [Exod. 2:1]; Elijah conducts sacrifice [I Kings 18:32 ff.]) . At the lower end of the chronological scale, to mention only the most prominent possibilities in the classification of dual functionaries, one thinks of Jeremiah and Ezekiel, both of whom come out of priestly backgrounds (Jer. 1:1; Ezek. 1:3) and exhibit a prophetism patently extending, in some significant regards, the ancient dual form.[2] As a rule, the representatives of Yahwistic prophetism saw themselves allied to the priesthood as colleagues in a fundamentally common task, a fact which further defines and underscores the relationship of concern of the prophet to the cultus.[3]

Form-critical studies confirm the prophets' cultic orientation. Several shorter prophetic writings (among them Habakkuk, Nahum, and Joel) are now interpreted as having been produced out of cultic influence, in the liturgical style of the cult ritual.[4] Elsewhere throughout the recorded prophetic utterances there appear strong suggestions of conscious or unconscious adaptation of cultic ritual. But this relationship between prophet and cultus can best be illustrated in the form-critical example which follows.

The Role of Form Criticism

Form criticism has over the past few decades exercised an incalculable influence on the interpretation of the Old Testament. The ultimate originator of the form-critical method for both the New and Old Testaments was Hermann Gunkel. For our purposes we may pick up the form-critical story with Gunkel's work in the Psalter, where he distinguished three primary types of psalms—those of Thanksgiving (*Danklied*), Lament (*Klagelied*), and, Gunkel's unique find, the *Hymnus*. Here Gunkel demonstrated the collective apprehension characteristic of the third type and concluded that it originated in the cultus. If it was later a privately composed psalm—if, that is, certain psalms of the *Hymnus* type were in fact of private composition—they were composed on the pattern of the cultic psalm. Gunkel further noted certain characteristic stylistic features, such as liturgical use of the particle "for" (Hebrew: *ki*):

O give thanks to the Lord for he is good,
for his steadfast love endures forever. (Ps. 136:1.)

and the participial form of the verb employed in series:

to *him who did* thus and so [participle in Hebrew]
for his steadfast love endures forever [this refrain is repeated 26 times] (Ps. 136:4 ff.).

The original setting (*Sitz im Leben*) of the *Hymnus* was incontestably the cultus.

Gunkel's highly influential *Einleitung in die Psalmen* appeared in 1933, a year after his death. It was completed and seen through the press by his brilliant pupil, J. Begrich, who in the following year, 1934, himself published an article of decisive importance in the development of form criticism and in the understanding and interpretation of prophetism. The article was entitled "Das priesterliche Heilsorakel"; that is, "The Priestly Oracle of Assurance." [5] The psalm of lament, the *Klagelied,* of the individual is characterized by a sudden change of mood toward the close of the psalm.[6] As a rule, in this type of psalm the psalmist first makes his bitter complaint and then follows it with an earnest request. Now the mood of the psalm suddenly changes, and the psalmist expresses his own assurance that the request has been granted and, usually, concludes the psalm with a vow of some sort on a very positive note. Begrich raised in his article the old question, What produced the sudden change of mood? He affirmed the old answer: Possibly and probably an oracle pronounced by an attendant priest in which Yahweh reassured the supplicant and granted his request. But Begrich, for the first time, attempted a reconstruction of this heretofore hypothetical oracle—with impressive results. The second Isaiah has, he concluded, deliberately employed the priestly oracle of assurance as the most appropriate form for his own message. The prophet has shaped his own prophetic preaching along lines literally dictated by a ritual form in common use in the pre-exilic temple. The priest's oracle is appropriate to the prophet's use because the prophet confronts a lamenting people as the priest confronted an indidividual in lament.

As reconstructed by Begrich from the words of Second Isaiah, with an occasional assist outside, the priestly oracle usually began with the words, "Fear thou not" (Isa. 41:10, 13, 14; 43:1, 5; 44:2; 51:7; 54:4; cf. Jer. 30:10 ff.=46:27 ff.), a fact supported by Lam. 3:57:

> Thou didst come near when I called on thee:
> thou didst say, "Fear thou not!"

This was sometimes followed in the oracle with the designation of the person addressed, and then, characteristically, a statement such as, "for I am with thee" (Isa. 41:10) ; "for I am thy God" (Jer. 30:10 and 46:27) ; or "for I am thy helper" (see further Isa. 43:5; Jer. 30:11; cf. also Isa. 41:13; 43:13; 48:17). Such sentences in the priest's oracle elicit corresponding statements from the supplicant in his concluding expression of assurance in the *Klagelied,* as, for example, "thou art my God" (Ps. 140:7) ; "my treasure and my fortress art thou" (Ps. 31:4).

The oracle then answers specifically the earnest requests of the supplicant, pleas such as the following:

> How long, Yahweh, wilt thou forget me forever? (Ps. 13:1.)
> Let them be put to shame and dishonor
>   who seek after my life!
> Let them be turned back and confounded
>   who devise evil against me. (Ps. 35:4; but cf. also Ps. 25:3;
>   31:18: 35:5, 26; 40:15 ff.; 63:10 ff.; 71:13; 83:13; 109:28 ff.;
>   119:78.)

> Let me not be put to shame. (Ps. 25:2; 31:2, 18; 69:7; 71:3; 119:6, 31, 46, 116; cf. Jer. 17:17.)

Such entreaties are reassuringly met in the priestly oracle with statements of this sort:

> For the moth will eat them up like a garment
> and the worm will eat them like wool. (Isa. 51:8.)
> Kings shall see and arise
> princes, and they shall prostrate themselves (49:7.)
> You will not be ashamed . . . you will not be put to shame
> you will forget the shame of your youth. (Isa. 54:4. Cf. Jer. 30:10 ff.)

Or the oracle simply assures the supplicant in general terms that all is well, with statements which suit as well the prophet's ministry to a people in exile as the priest's ministry in the temple to individuals in private anguish. Help has already been given, and Begrich underlines the fact that the verb is in the perfect (not, as R.S.V., future) tense:

> I have strengthened you, I have helped you
> I have upheld you with my victorious right hand. (Isa. 41:10.)
> I have called you by name. You are mine. (Isa. 43:1; see 41:14; 54:8.)

The tense distinction is important. Yahweh assures the supplicant through the priest's oracle that he has heard and that the need has been decisively met, and the supplicant, taking his cue from the oracle, speaks now with absolute assurance in the perfect tense, as if the satisfaction of his complaints were already a *fait accompli:*

> Thou hast smitten all my enemies on the cheek
> Thou hast broken the teeth of the wicked. (Ps. 3:7.)

The oracle of the priest may add, to the assurances put in the perfect tense, a series of imperfects, making certain guarantees for the future:

When [Hebrew: *ki*] you pass [impf.] through the waters I will
    be with you
[The conditional quality of speech is clearer in the German translations: *Gehst du durch Wasser, so bin ich bei dir.*]
    And through the rivers, they shall not overwhelm you.
When you walk through fire you shall not be burned
    And the flame shall not consume you. (Isa. 43:2.)

This combination of tenses, the joining of the imperfect to the perfect, is echoed again by the supplicant when he resumes the psalm following the delivery of the priestly oracle:

> Depart from me, all you workers of evil;
>   for Yahweh has heard the sound of my weeping.
> Yahweh has heard my supplication
>   Yahweh accepts my prayer.
> All my enemies shall be ashamed and sorely troubled.
>   They shall turn back and be put to shame in a
>   moment. (Ps. 6:8-10 [Hebrew: vss. 9-11].)

After pointing out ways in which the simple form of the priestly oracle of assurance is expanded in prophetic use

Begrich shows further close connections between the priestly oracle and the psalm of lament. If the supplicant cries, "I am thy servant" (Ps. 143:12; cf. 19:12; 27:9; 31:17; 69:18; 86:2; 4, 16; 109:28; 119:17, 38), it is acknowledged by Yahweh in the oracle:

> You Israel, my servant . . . to whom I said,
>> You are my servant. (Isa. 41:8-9; cf. 44:1; Jer. 30:10=46:27.)

If the supplicant in his misery calls himself a worm (Ps. 22:7; cf. Job 25:6), one who is despised by the people (Ps. 22:7; cf. 119:141), or a mockery of the people (Ps. 22:7; Job 30:10), the priestly oracle picks up these phrases and uses them to let the supplicant know that Yahweh has in fact been moved by his pitiable condition:

> Fear not, you worm Jacob. (Isa. 41:14.)
> Thus says Yahweh to one deeply despised, abhorred by the people. (Isa. 49:7; cf. 51:7: 54:8.)

In response to the very frequent expression of anxiety and fear in the *Klagelied* (e.g., 31:14; 38:19; 55:4; 61:3; 64:2; 69:18; 86:16; 102:3) we meet the repeated consoling words of the divine answer "You shall have no fear" (Isa. 41:10, 13, 14; 43:1, 5; 44:2; 51:7; 54:4; Lam. 3:57; Jer. 30:10 ff.= 46:27 ff.). To the despairing cry, "My God, my God, why hast thou forsaken me?" (Ps. 22:1 [Hebrew: vs. 2]) comes the answer, "For a brief moment only have I forsaken you." Isa. 54:7.) To the shaken outcry, "How long, Yahweh, wilt thou forget me forever?" (Ps. 13:1 [Hebrew: vs. 2]), the divine word responds through the priest's oracle:

Can a woman forget her sucking child? . . .
Even these may forget; but I will not forget you! (Isa. 49:15.)

This thesis by Begrich has gained wide acceptance, and it speaks eloquently of the relationship of prophet and priest, of prophet and cultus. As Begrich himself pointed out, "The prophet claims for his message the same authority and the same demand of faith which the priestly *Heilsorakel* claimed in the cultus and to which the supplicant willingly responded."

To entertain reservations as to the great prophets' membership in the guilds of professional cult prophets is in no sense at all, then, to cut the prophet off from influencial and productive interrelationship in the cult. Far from repudiating the cultus, the prophet as exemplified in Second Isaiah can and does appropriate the liturgy in common use in the daily round of cultic exercise and, again in the case of Second Isaiah, make frequent appeal to familiar lines in the common ritual in the repeated words, "Have you not known, have you not heard . . ." (Isa. 40:21, 28). The prophet must not be removed from his own original environment, his own broadly contemporaneous setting.

Prophet and Book

The old interpretation of the classical prophet, the "name" prophet, as a grandly isolated figure has been attacked and largely routed from yet another quarter. Well into the twentieth century the most common designation of the great prophets was the term, "writing prophets," used to distinguish prophets with "book" from those without. Elijah was a prophet. Amos was a writing prophet. It was taken for granted that writings bearing prophetic names contained for the most part the actual written words of the prophet. Or, to say the same thing and make the same distinction, the "writing" prophets were "literary" prophets—they habitually addressed themselves, pen in hand as it were, to the blank scroll. Following an address (e.g., Amos' speech at Bethel) they carefully cast the utterance into written form themselves being "literary" men. Of years later, they looked back on an event, experience, or speech (e.g., Isaiah upon his call) and "put it down on paper," themselves "reducing" the remembered episode to writing. This firm assumption that the books of the prophets were, by and large, handwritten by the great prophets themselves from the eighth to the sixth centuries (Amos-Second Isaiah) may be seen in interpretations of the prophets which in other respects represent remarkably different perspectives.

As Old Testament scholarship turned into the second half of this century the earlier easy assumption of the literary activity of the "book" prophets gave way before an increasing emphasis—exaggerated to be sure in some quarters—on the role of oral composition and transmission and the relationship of at least some of these prophets to circles of disciples. In a pattern demonstrated in great variety over the whole of the ancient Near East, the great prophet played the role of master among a number of more or less formally organized disciples. Responsibility for the original, basic—oral—form of the present prophetic writings came to be fixed upon these disciples who cherished, preserved, and "edited" the utterances of the master, not only during the prophet's lifetime, but for an extended period of time after his death. The present written form of prophetic speech may be analyzed, assessed, and interpreted only in consideration of its significant history as oral formalization and entity.

Form criticism underscores the role of oral tradition by demonstrating that much of profoundest meaning in the Old Testament is closely related to a continuing cultic activity which was largely sustained by the mouth and memory of successive generations of participants. Form criticism shatters the common assumption in the "literate" West that books and documents are created only by writers. The Old Testament, form-critically regarded, is much more the creation of speaking worshipers and remembering worshipers. The past is orally appropriated in the present, and the community—past, present, and future—is centrally oriented in a common cultus. In highlighting the real context of Israel's actual historical existence, form criticism confronts us repeatedly with the fact that in the ancient East the role of written transmission, while significantly existent, remained sometimes, and for long periods of time, subordinate to that of oral transmission.

Studies in comparative culture in the ancient Near East, especially by Scandinavian scholars, give further emphasis— sometimes exaggerated—to the place of oral tradition. One is hardly justified in saying that the written Old Testament "is a creation of the post-exilic Jewish community; of what existed earlier undoubtedly only a small part was in fixed written form." [7] This is certainly going too far. The writing of history and tradition in Israel increased in impressive proportion from the tenth century B.C. At the same time, one must insist on the continuing interrelationship between parallel written and oral formulation and transmission of material and, in the case of certain types—including the utterances of the great prophets—on the dominant but not exclusive oral organization and preservation of the material down to the Exile in the sixth century.

There can be no doubt that at least some of the "book" prophets lived and taught and proclaimed a message in the company of disciples. Nor can the function of oral transmission among these disciples be eliminated in the history of the organization and preservation of prophetic utterance in the Old Testament. The real question is simply that of evaluating what is received. To what extent, for example, do we find the man and the prophet Isaiah in what is now recorded in the book of Isaiah? To what extent is the content of the prophetic book the product of the machinery of transmission? This is of course to ask the question, What is the relationship between the "book" prophet and the book, between the prophet and his disciples, between the disciples and the book? Have we been wrong for well over two thousand years now in assuming that the book of Amos or of Jeremiah reflects the mind, personality, and utterance of the prophet Amos, the prophet Jeremiah? Shall we say with certain scholars that we can never regain the actual words (the *ipsissima verba*) of Old Testament personalities, or that any hard and fast distinction between what comes from the prophet himself and what had its origin in subsequent tradition is no longer possible? [8]

The image of the great prophet as an absolutely solitary figure who is himself his own community and his own only scribe is wrong. Probably wrong too is the assumption that the form in which we now receive the words of the prophets is with any consistency the form in which it was initially cast by the prophet's own hand. Conversely, the evidence hardly justifies the conclusion that no prophet ever wrote anything himself, that we cannot make contact with and define an individual prophet because what is represented as his is in its indistinguishable entirety a traditio-historical creation, the product of decades and even centuries of a fluid, oral process.

In the case of Isaiah there is the strongest evidence both that the prophet himself wrote, and that on occasion he committed his message for subsequent delivery in oral form to a circle of disciples. In Isa. 8:1 we read:

> Then Yahweh said to me,
> "Take a large tablet and write
>   upon it in common characters,
>   'Belonging to Maher-shalal-hash-baz.' "

And in Isa. 30:8:

> And now, go,
> Write it before them on a tablet
> and inscribe it in a book,
> that it may be for the time to come
> as a witness for ever.

Further support is inferential. It is, for example, most improbable—in fact most inconceivable—that Isaiah was illiter-

ate, whether or not, as has often been surmised, he was a
member of the royalty of Jerusalem.

That there was also oral communication, transmission,
and preservation of the words of Isaiah through a circle of
disciples is made explicit in the text of Isaiah and is confirmed in Second Isaiah.

> Bind up the testimony,
> seal the teaching among my disciples [He-
> brew: *limmudim*]
> I will wait for Yahweh,
> who is hiding his face from the house of
> Jacob
> and I will hope in him. (8:16-17.)

The message thus sealed among Isaiah's disciples—the message, presumably, of the ultimate redemption of Israel—is
identified and publicly brought forth some two centuries
later by Second Isaiah, who also identifies himself as a par-
ticipant and member in that—still continuing—discipleship
to Isaiah of Jerusalem.

> The Lord Yahweh has given me the tongue of
> those-who-are-taught [Hebrew "disciples":
> *limmudim*]
> that I may know how to sustain with a word
> him that is weary.
> Morning by morning he wakens,
> he wakens my ear
> to hear as those-who-are-taught [again "dis-
> ciples": *limmudim*]. (50:4.)

I myself have no hesitation in endorsing the interpretation of these words of Second Isaiah as the prophet's wish to make it clear that he, a child of a later age, numbered himself with the disciples of Isaiah and wished to be numbered with them.[9]

As more imprecise support for a circle of discipleship to Isaiah, one calls attention to the nature of the present book of Isaiah, the remarkable unity pervading its various major sections (including not only chs. 40-55, but 56-66 and 24-27) and, within chs. 1-39, the continuing debate as to the "authenticity" of numbers of passages, chapters, and sections. In view of the undeniable span of several centuries embraced by the present book of Isaiah one suspects that the very book in its present form testifies to a long-continuing discipleship to the first Isaiah, the Isaiah of eighth-century Jerusalem.

Isaiah's influence is of course widely felt in the Old Testament outside the book of Isaiah. Subsequent prophets betray Isaianic influence, resulting from a knowledge of Isaiah or "the Isaianic" as recorded in writing or in the living discipleship or both. The little book of Micah is especially interesting testimony. If chs. 1-3 may—with the possible exception of 2:12 ff.—be assigned to the prophet Micah (either writing himself or as recorded by his own disciples), we sense in the two sections that follow, chs. 4-5 and 6-7, a strong affinity with Isaiah and the circle of his disciples:

> But you, O Bethlehem Ephrathah [Birthplace of
> David: the reference is to the David-Zion cove-
> nant, characteristic of Isaiah]
> . . . from you shall come forth for me
> one who is to be ruler in Israel,

> Whose origin is from of old . . .
> Therefore he [Yahweh] shall give them [Judah] up
> until the time when she
> who is in travail has brought forth. . . .
> And he shall stand and feed his flock in the strength
> of Yahweh,
> In the majesty of the name of Yahweh his God. . . .
> (Mic. 5:2 ff.; cf. Isa. 9; 11; 40:11.)

> But as for me [Micah? Or a prophet from the Isaiah
> circle?]
> I will look to Yahweh
> I will wait for the God of my salvation. . . . (Mic.
> 6:7; cf. Isa 8:17, quoted above.)

We note also the eloquent anti-Assyrianism in Micah (see especially 5:10 ff.), strongly reminiscent even in language and vocabulary of the Isaianic circle. If some of this material is from Micah, or if it fairly represents what was in fact the prophetic mind of Micah, then we must deduce an effective relationship between Isaiah and Micah, and we are justified in thinking that Micah was known to the Isaiah circle and that he too held in faith the prophetic expectation of redemption beyond judgment.[10]

The affinity between the book of Micah and the Isaiah circle is further marked by the presence of an oracle, the so-called "floating oracle," common to both books. One hazards the guess that it is not from Micah, that it may originate with Isaiah, that in testimony to its living oracular form it appears in Mic. 4:1-3 in a form longer than that in Isa. 2:2-4 and that it is one more item in support and clarification of the phenomenon of prophetic discipleship and of the joint role of the oracular and the written in the transmission of the content of prophetism.

On the question of whether the formation and transmission of prophetic utterance was predominantly written or oral a distinction ought to be made between two types of canonical prophetism, the liturgical and the so-called *diwan* type. The former, strongly influenced by established and probably recorded liturgy, is represented in such books as Nahum, Habakkuk, Joel, and Second Isaiah. It was produced by writers and experienced a predominantly written tradition from the very beginning. The latter is seen in prophets like Amos and Isaiah of Jerusalem and comes down out of a process of transmission largely oral.[11]

Whatever the actual circumstances of the creation of the various components of prophetism, we must acknowledge the role of oral as well as written transmission. Oral and written forms of "prophecy" were no doubt simultaneously current. Oral communication was not necessarily less accurate, and certainly it was more widely and more popularly used than writing, at least down to the sixth century.[12] Even that which the prophet recorded with his own hand or directly through a disciple continued orally alive and was far more frequently communicated from tongue to ear than from scroll to eye. Finally, there is every reason to think that some of the great prophets' preaching and teaching achieved written form only after sustained oral life among the disciples of the prophets.

NOTES

[1] So also Sigmund Mowinckel, *Psalmenstudien, II: Das Thronbesteigungsfest Jahwäs und der Ursprung der Eschatologie* (Kristiania, 1922), pp. 315 ff., "The cult always contained a forward look."

[2] A. Jepsen, *Nabi* (Munich, 1934), probably goes too far in distinguishing between Yahwistic prophetism in North and South but he very properly points to the fact of frequent mention of priest, temple, and sacrifice in reports of the activities of prophets in Judah (I Sam. 2:27 ff.; II Sam. 24; 7; I Kings 1; 13; II Kings 18-20) and that "in thirty passages priest and prophet are cited in association" (p. 161), passages listed in note 2.

[3] Cf. R. B. Y. Scott, *The Relevance of the Prophets* (New York: The Macmillan Company, 1947), p. 42 ff.

[4] P. Humbert, *Problems du livre d'Habacuc* (Neuchatel, 1944); A. Haldar, *Studies in the Book of Nahum* (Uppsala, 1946); A. S. Kapelrud, *Joel Studies* (Uppsala, 1948).

[5] *Zeitschrift für die alttestamentlichen Wissenschaft* (1934), 52, 81-92.

[6] According to Gunkel, *Einleitung in die Psalmen* (Göttingen, 1933), p. 172, the following psalms belong to this type (*die Klagelieder des Einzelnen*): 3, 5, 6, 7, 13, 17, 22, 25, 27:7-14, 28, 31, 35, 39, 42, 43, 51, 54-57, 59, 61, 63, 64, 69, 70, 71, 76, 88, 102, 109, 120, 130, 140-43 and, also belonging to this type, Lam. 3.

[7] H. S. Nyberg, *Studien zum Hoseabuche* (1935), p. 8; as quoted by Eduard Nielsen, *Oral Tradition* (Toronto: Ryerson Press, 1954) (No. 11 in the series *Studies in Biblical Theology*), p. 39.

[8] See now the illuminating discussion by Eissfeldt, "The Prophetic Literature," Rowley, *The Old Testament and Modern Study*, pp. 128 ff.

[9] Martin Buber, *The Prophetic Faith* (New York: The Macmillan Company, 1949), pp. 203 ff.: " 'Disciples tongue' it was, because his task was to uncover the master's words as a consolation and succour." See also pp. 147 ff.; and cf. A. Bentzen, *Introduction to the Old Testament* (2 vols.; Copenhagen, 1952), II, 108, who takes for granted a continuing "circle of disciples" to Isaiah.

[10] Against Von Rad who remarks what appears to him to be a critical difference in the two prophets' appropriation of Israel's old traditions. Hosea, he says, takes his stand on the old Israel-Covenant theology while Isaiah "appears not even once to be familiar with it and professes exclusively the Zion-David tradition" *Theologie,* I, 74. This may be, although I am not at all convinced of Isaiah's ignorance of—or even his disposition to ignore—the older Exodus covenant (e.g., Isa. 1:2-3). In any case subsequent Isaianic tradition combines the two covenants of Exodus and David-Zion, and the demonstrable affinity of Hosea and Isaiah as presently formulated remains. Cf. also Von Rad, *Theologie,* II, 158 ff.

[11] So Engnell, *The Call of Isaiah,* pp. 59 ff.:

By no means do we have to reckon exclusively with oral tradition. . . . Personally I have . . . tried to typologize the so-called "prophetical literature" in two main groups: *"The liturgical type"* ("liturgy" taken as a purely form-literary term) to be found in Nah., Hab., Joel, "Deuter-Isa," *et al.,* with real "writers" behind them, and probably from the very beginning taken down in writing, and *"the diwan type"* (no very good term, I admit), e.g., Am., Proto-Isa., etc., primarily resting on oral transmission. . . .

In further support of the role of writing, I strongly endorse the words of G. Widengren, *Literary and Psychological Aspects of the Hebrew Prophets* (Uppsala, 1948), p. 77:

In the case of the three great prophets Isaiah, Jeremiah and Ezekiel there is a mention of their writing down or dictating their prophecies. *All of them surely wrote down at least part of their prophecies, that much is incontrovertible* [italics his]. . . . How the prophetic texts of an Amos or a Hosea were transmitted, we do not know. But in view of the excellent state of the text of Amos and the comparatively good condition of that of Hosea we are not much inclined to assume that their prophecies have been handed down exclusively by means of oral tradition.

[12] See now the study by Nielsen, *op. cit.*

III

Pre-prophetic "Prophets"

AN ESSENTIAL PROPHETISM WAS PRESENT IN ANCIENT ISRAEL long before the rise and development of the classical prophetic moment of the eighth and following centuries. A core tradition of Yahwism, in the broad sense certainly "prophetic," was maintained in a fluid continuum from Moses to Malachi. The expression of the characteristically prophetic bent of mind occurred among the Old Testament people long in advance of classical prophetism. This is to say, then, that the classical prophet, although highly creative and proclaiming a new word, was debtor, and certainly conscious debtor, to a core tradition already long established.[1] This is also to say that one must of necessity define the essentially prophetic quality in pre-Amos Israel by the standards of classical prophetism, and further that no history, and perhaps least of all biblical history, may be appropriated in sterile chronological fashion. The past of a people, or any aspect of that people's past, must be interpreted in the light of what that past becomes.[2] Not that we have or will ever have full knowledge of the phenomenon of classical prophetism, but that the emerging form of prophetism in early Israel may be addressed, apprehended, and assessed only against what we may know, rationally and intuitively, of the matured phenomenon.

Prophetic Essence: Address to History

Old Testament prophetism will no doubt continue to be a subject of vigorous debate. On one point, however, there is no possibility of dispute. *The characteristically prophetic phenomenon always presupposes the decisive impingement of Yahweh upon history.* This is true whether the prophetic word be invective or judgment, assurance or promise, cry of anguish or confession. This is true whether the prophetic act be concrete, symbolic, or relational. This is true whether the presupposition that Yahweh determines history be conscious or unconscious, explicit or taken for granted, immediately relevant or only of indirect ultimate pertinence. Where this sense of the effective relationship of Yahweh to history is absent prophetism is also absent. Where this is present, where without this sense of the interrelatedness of history and deity the utterance, the situation, the personality, or the relationship would be radically altered—there is prophetism.

Premonarchic "Prophets"

Down to the eighth century the term "prophet" appears linked to the names of a considerable number of persons. Five prominent names from premonarchic times are by tradition attached to the title: Abraham (Gen. 20:7), Aaron (Exod. 7:1), Miriam and Deborah (both *nebi'ah,* fem., *nabi';* Exod. 15:20 and Judg. 4:4), and Moses (Deut. 34:10; 18:18; cf. Num. 11:26-29; 12:5-8). The term was hardly then in use among the Israelites. The word *nabi'* came to be applied to Israelite functionaries in the tenth century, and in the later classical sense of the term, sometime during or after

Amos' day. The term as a title applied to these individuals can hardly originate earlier than the latter part of the ninth century, and much more likely reflects the development of tradition in the eighth or seventh century. It is nevertheless interesting and instructive that these five are awarded the title. The patriarchal saga tends noticeably to impute to Abraham a sense of divinely ordained history which in Israel could only be post-Exodus.[3] A man who, as remembered in tradition, can in faith (Gen. 15:6) accept the divine promises detailed in Gen. 12:1-3, 7; a man who, in that same tradition, not only stands in awareness of Yahweh's radically purposive impingement on history, but also understands himself in an absolutely central role therein—such a man profoundly deserves the ascription "prophet."

Aaron's case is less significant but also instructive.

> And Yahweh said to Moses
> "See, I make you as God to Pharaoh;
> And Aaron your brother
> shall be your prophet." (Exod. 7:1, P.)

Again the linking by later tradition of the name with the title presupposes the understanding of prophetism in fundamental terms of Yahweh's efficacious relationship to history. It further conveys the definition of prophet as one who articulates the meaning of the divine impingement from a remarkably knowledgeable position. This interpretation is confirmed and elaborated in Exod. 4:14 ff. [4] when Yahweh responds with some heat to Moses' protest that he is no speaker:

60

Is there not Aaron . . . ?
I know that he can speak well. . . .
And you shall speak to him
   and put the words in his mouth. . . .
He shall speak for you to the people;
   and he shall be a mouth for you,
   and you shall be to him as God.

To Miriam tradition ascribes, correctly or incorrectly, the composition of the lines which, with brilliant economy, convey the whole prophetic theology of the Exodus: [5]

Sing to Yahweh,
   for he has triumphed gloriously;
The horse and his rider
   he has thrown into the sea!

Equally appropriately, tradition names Deborah a prophet. The "Song of Deborah" (Judg. 5) conveys a premonarchic, if not contemporary, interpretation of a victory of Yahweh and a number of Israelite tribes over a Canaanite coalition sometime around 1100 B.C. Thus Deborah no less than Miriam is represented in celebration of what Yahweh is doing in concrete relationship to the historical existence of Israel.

In the case of Moses, it is instructive that J, the earliest Old Testament historical "source," [6] nowhere accords him the title "prophet." J does not call Moses a prophet because the term is not so employed in Israel in the Yahwist's day. It is another matter in E, however, which reflects the century between 850 and 750 B.C. The entire E material probably

61

stems from early prophetic circles, and where it deals with Moses it reflects consistently the conviction that he is a prophet, and the greatest of the prophets.

And there has not arisen a prophet since in Israel like Moses, whom Yahweh knew face to face, none like him for all the signs and the wonders which Yahweh sent him to do in the land of Egypt . . . and for all the mighty power and all the great and terrible deeds which Moses wrought in the sight of all Israel. (Deut. 34:10 ff., E.) [8]

The prophetism which Moses represents is of a special sort; he is the performing prophet, actively intervening in events. In this Moses towers above all other prophets (Num. 12: 7 ff.). If the qualities of mediation and intercession are here (Exod. 18:19; 32:11-13; Num. 12:11), these qualities are heightened, augmented in the extreme. In order to save Israel, Moses is prepared to become anathema on behalf of his people (Exod. 32:32; cf. Rom. 9:3).[9]

In the Deuteronomic perspective Moses is the ideal prophet. In Deut. 18:18 he reports what Yahweh has told him: "I will raise up for them a prophet like you from among their brethren; and I will put my words in his mouth, and he shall speak to them all that I command him." A change has occurred in the century or so separating E and D. With D in the seventh century emphasis has passed from the prophet's deed to the prophet's word. While the role of the prophet has been altered, however, the central character of prophetism is the same—namely, concern with and the demonstration of the critical impingement of divine life upon human history.

Moses acquires the title "prophet" by retrojection. In identifying Moses as a prophet, E and D inform us not so much about the man Moses in the thirteenth century as about the best expectations for the prophet in the eighth and the seventh centuries. We may agree that the historical Moses appropriately heads the list of Old Testament prophets as prophetism is broadly defined and that E and D were not wrong in making the identification. For our present purposes, however, the great question of the "historical Moses" must be considered of secondary importance. The real issue is to comprehend the true nature and function of prophetism in ancient Israel. The impression of Moses which is ours from the biblical narrative is already prophetically interpreted (even in the Yahwist, since we shall presently see the Yahwist himself as an early historical figure in the total movement of prophetism). This is a Moses who lived in prophetic experience in Israel not as a figure of the past but as the first of a line of prophets who in the present are continuing to bring Israel up from Egypt into existence under God.[10]

The primary effort to recover an exclusively pragmatic historical past in ancient Israel is always doomed, and more than that, it is, as effort, in error. The time span between the given "present" and the appropriated past varies widely, from the relatively narrow gap between David and the account of him in II Sam. 9-20 plus I Kings 1-2 to the recreation of Moses in the Deuteronomic corpus and, still later, the priestly writing. But in the Old Testament we have no past which has not already been appropriated in a subsequent present, and so appropriated as to *be* in the present, to *live* in the present. If the "historical Moses" is irrecoverable for this reason, so is the "historical Exodus"—it *was* past, but it now *is*. The event lives in faith. It has beeen culticized. It is as such, psychologically speaking, not so much merely memorialized as re-experienced—created and lived again. Moses and the Exodus and all of Israel's recorded past are received by us in a form of penetrating and consistent "is-ness," and there exists therefore no way whatsoever to effect a concrete recovery of the now totally silent and absent "wasness." Prophetism is to confront man with God-in-history. It is timelessly the bringing of Israel, *always now,* up from Egypt into existence under God! So *is* Moses a prophet.

The Yahwist as Prophet

This is something else. As an entity so termed we predicate a man, an individual. We presume further to place him within rather narrow limits of time, considering the relative antiquity of his epoch—i.e., before the death of Solomon and, at the earliest, the final years of David's reign. We predicate, in addition, a historian—no mere chronicler of the past, but one who addresses and is overwhelmingly addressed by the present, who is impressed with what is for him the indelible meaning of the present, who comprehends that meaning as the existent form of Israel, and who, in order to articulate that form, spontaneously expands its meaning into a past already present and, in rare, involuntary bursts, into a future equally present but relatively imperceptible.[11]

The Yahwist is known to us not as one who, like Moses, is appropriated from the past, but as himself an appropriator of the past. His work, which constitutes the basic structure of

the Hexateuch, is all that we know of him. It is a creative
production whose creativity inheres, not in verbal, but in
structural composition. By and large he reproduces what has
already earlier been produced and achieves by inspired selec-
tion, juxtaposition, and broadly conceived arrangement of
varied existent traditional materials an artistically and theo-
logically unified "history." His total achievement is a brilliant, highly coherent definition of the essential form of
Israel, a form apprehended in a continuum of meaning from
the present to the past and back to the present again. If the
irrecoverable and undefinable, but certainly historical, thir-
teenth-century Moses was among the prophets, as his easy
appropriation thereto would lead us to suspect, he is followed
in the prophetic succession (and who is to say how many
"prophets" may have come between?) [12] by this nameless
untitled prophet who is known to us only by the divine name
(the Yahwist, from Yahweh), this tenth-century proclaimer
of Yahweh's critical impingement upon history, this prophetic delineator of Israel's form and meaning in terms of emergence from Egypt into existence under God.

The Yahwist sees, and through the form and structure of
his work proclaims, such an impingement of the divine life
upon history as cannot be contained by the life of Israel. The
effects spill upon all men and nations, in all time. It is,
therefore, quite wrong to argue that Hellenism created the
idea of ecumenical history. [13] The Greek language and Hel-
lenistic culture provided the term and a specialized content,
but ecumenicity already inhered, if in quietness and sublety,
in some ancient Israel's earliest stories. It gained its first emphatic description of meaning, long before the origin of the

mere term, in the Yahwist's work. The J opus proclaims Yahweh's impingement on Israel, to be sure, but at once—such is the historical form of Israel and its dependent meaning—upon the world, the whole household of God. The primeval history (the Yahwist's material in Gen. 2-11) and its structural relationship to the story of Abraham and all that follows testifies to the Yahwist's sweeping ecumenical perspective.[14]

The Yahwist's place in the broad tradition of Israelite prophetism is sure. Acknowledgment of the Yahwist as "prophet" renders the more comprehensible the roles in prophetism of Samuel, Nathan, and Elijah, as well as the classical prophets from Amos to Second Isaiah.

NOTES

[1] See further G. H. Davies, "The Yahwistic Tradition in the Eighth-Century Prophets," *Studies in Old Testament Prophecy,* edited by H. H. Rowley (Edinburgh: T. & T. Clark, 1950), pp. 37-51. Cf. also von Rad *Theologie des Alten Testaments* (Munich, 1957), II, pp. 20-26.

[2] "A discussion of the emergence of form entails a knowledge of a civilization in its maturity, a familiarity with its classical expression in every field." Henri Frankfort, *The Birth of Civilization in the Near East* (Garden City, N. Y.: Doubleday & Company, 1956), p. 25.

[3] See further B. D. Napier, *From Faith to Faith* (New York: Harper & Row, Publishers, 1955), pp. 60-71.

[4] Conventionally assigned to the E document (representing eighth-seventh century?).

[5] F. Cross and N. Freedman have argued that the long poem preceding Exod. 15:21 is the "Song of Miriam" and scarcely later than the twelfth

century in its original form. See "Song of Miriam," *Journal of Near Eastern Studies*, Vol. xiv, No. 4 (October, 1955).

⁶ "Source" criticism ran its full, complex course in the latter half of the preceding century and the early years of the present century. A solid core still stands out of that massive structure. This includes, at least for me, the integrity of J as a documentary entity, representing the brilliant, creative editorial work of an individual whom we call the Yahwist. This work of the Yahwist, J, drew from older sources (and probably chiefly from a pre-J collection of traditional materials) and dates from the tenth century. Adequate grounds have never existed for the repudiation of D and P as sources. E continues to require symbolization, whether or not it ever existed as a separate and roughly parallel source to J, as simply that hexateuchal material differing from or later than J but earlier than D or P. Cf. Gerhard von Rad, *Genesis*, translated by John H. Marks (from *Das erste Buch Mose*) in the series *Das Alte Testament Deutsch, II* (Göttingen, 1953; Philadelphia: The Westminster Press, 1961), pp. 23 ff. and 27 ff. (German: pp. 16 ff. and 20 ff.). The reader may also be interested in seeing my fuller, but summary, discussion in *Song of the Vineyard* (New York: Harper & Row, Publishers, 1962), pp. 25-27 and footnotes p. 26.

⁷ Von Rad, *Theologie*, I, 292.

⁸ Robert H. Pfeiffer, *Introduction to the Old Testament* (New York: Harper & Brothers, 1941), p. 175.

⁹ Von Rad, *Theologie*, I, 292, almost verbatim.

¹⁰ So, substantially, Eric Voegelin, *Israel and Revelation* (Baton Rouge, La.: Louisiana State University Press, 1956), p. 428.

¹¹ Cf. Robin George Collingwood, *The Idea of History* (New York: Oxford University Press, 1946); Frankfort, *op. cit.;* and Voegelin, *op. cit.*, especially Chap. 4, "Israel and History."

¹² If, as seems probable, a prophet-theologian earlier than the Yahwist first brought together the bulk of material now assigned to J, he too must take his place in this succession.

¹³ Collingwood, *op. cit.*, p. 32.

¹⁴ See now especially Von Rad, *Genesis*, p. 22 ff. (German: p. 15 ff.). Because the passage in Von Rad is crucial to what I am trying to say, and

because it is in my judgment still the best interpretive statement on the
primeval story in Genesis, I presume to give here my own translation, indicating and/or retaining a few of the key German terms employed by Von
Rad:

The structure of the primeval history, which the Yahwist put together from a
highly varied assortment of materials, proclaims . . . . with magnificent singleness
of aim that all corruption, all disorder (*Wirrnis*) in the world is the result of sin;
and yet at the same time it also bears witness that to the steadily widening breach
between God and man there corresponds an inherently powerful expression of
grace. The accounts of the Fall, of Cain, and of Noah, also and unmistakably reflect
God's forgiving and sustaining concern for man (*Heilshandeln*). Only in the Babel
story, with the dispersion of peoples and the loss of human unity, does the judgment
of God appear to be the final word. But here the primeval history (*Urgeschichte*)
is merged with the story of salvation (*Heilsgeschichte*): Abraham is called out of the
multitude of peoples, "that in him all the families of the earth may be blessed." Thus
at the very outset, *Heilsgeschichte* replies to the unanswered question of *Urgeschichte*,
the question of God's relationship to all peoples together. This point where *Heilsgeschichte* sets in, Gen. 12:1-3, is at once the conclusion of the *Urgeschichte* and the
only key to its interpretation. In this fusion of *Urgeschichte* and *Heilsgeschichte*
the Yahwist makes articulate the meaning and aim of the role in the history of
salvation which Yahweh has granted Israel. He gives the etiology of all etiologies in
the Old Testament and in doing so assumes the true status of a prophet: on grounds
supported neither rationally nor by particulars he proclaims the spanning of the
chasm between God and all mankind as God's ultimate, saving, goal to be effected
through Israel. The promise in Gen. 12:1 ff. contains a threefold assurance of good-
ness: 1) Abraham will be blessed and become a great people. 2) Yahweh will give
the land to the seed of Abraham (12:7). 3) in Abraham all branches of the human
family will be blessed (12:3). The first two promises were given the Yahwist in
patriarchal tradition; but the third obviously has its origin in none of the ancient
traditions but precisely in the authenticity (*Vollmacht*) of his prophetic inspiration.

IV

Prophets to Kings:
The Tenth and Ninth Centuries

SIX PARTICULARLY IMPORTANT PROPHETIC FIGURES APPEAR IN
these two centuries. To all of them the term "prophet" is
applied—Samuel, whose career begins, of course, in the
eleventh century; Nathan, and Ahijah in the tenth century;
Elijah, Micaiah, and Elisha in the ninth.

Their Role in Prophetism

The institution of prophetism as a group phenomenon
had its origins in Israel immediately before and during the
creation of the monarchy. The first specifically Israelite application of the term *nabiʾ*, prophet, was no doubt to members of such groups (I Sam. 10). If I Sam. 19:18-24 is authentic in suggesting Samuel's integral relationship to such
a group, Samuel may have been known as a prophet in his
own time. This is uncertain, however. With rare exception,
he is represented as a singular figure, functioning in the
fashion of a judge, priest, or seer. When a narrator tells us in
I Sam. 9:9 that although Samuel was known as a seer *then,*
we should now (in the narrator's somewhat later time) call
him a prophet, we assume that Samuel was never primarily
identified with the early Israelite institution of group
prophecy and was not commonly, if at all, so termed by his

contemporaries. This interpretation runs counter to the oftentimes prevailing view of Samuel, that he is what he is predominantly as a result of his membership in the associated prophetism of the day. There can be no doubt, of course, that Samuel was in accord with the radical political implications of these early prophets' fierce loyalty to Yahweh, that he was allied with them in setting up the monarchy, and that there was mutual influence between Samuel and the emerging prophetic institution. But the whole Samuel cannot thus be explained and/or dismissed.

David brought the institution of prophetism into the court, on how large a scale we do not know. If his prophet Nathan consistently appears in a singular role, Nathan's official status and title, "prophet," is derived from a prophetism thus institutionalized, and perhaps in the court initially institutionalized only in the person of Nathan. The regularity and varying contexts of the designation "Nathan the prophet" suggests an official title, as does the repeated coupling of the phrase with other officially titled persons in I Kings 1.

Ahijah, who is called a prophet in I Kings 11:29; 14:2, 18, was commonly known as Ahijah the Shilonite (I Kings 11:29; 12:15; II Chr. 9:29; 10:15; cf. also I Kings 14:4). We do not question the appropriateness of the term as applied to him, but, on the example of Samuel and Nathan, we suspect that if he was called a prophet by his contemporaries it was, again, because of regularized status as a professional, in this case presumably membership in an association of prophets at or near Shiloh.

In the comparable case of Elijah the evidence is strongly

against his having been in his own day commonly termed a prophet, and we suspect the same of Ahijah. Neither prophet, we think, was identified with any form of professional prophetic organization, and neither was consequently so termed. In the Elijah texts (I Kings 17-19; 21; II Kings 1-2) the name Elijah occurs alone except in I Kings 17:1; 21:17; and 21:28 (the last is certainly secondary) and II Kings 1:3, 8 (which is also from later narrators than the original basic story of I Kings 17-19; 21).[1] In all these it is "Elijah the Tishbite" as in the preceding century it was "Ahijah the Shilonite." "Elijah the prophet" occurs only in I Kings 18:36, and most commentators believe "the prophet" is probably a later gloss. In I Kings 18:22: "Elijah said to the people, 'I, even I only, am left a prophet of Yahweh; but Baal's prophets are four hundred and fifty men.'" In I Kings 19:14 (also vs. 10, but by error from vs. 14) Elijah bitterly protests that: "the people of Israel have . . . slain thy prophets with the sword; and I, even I only, am left; and they seek my life to take it away." The narrator gives Elijah professional status when he appears in the narrative (I Kings 18:22) in opposition to the group-functioning prophets of Baal and by a process of sympathetic identification, when the banded Yahweh prophets are being persecuted by the aggressive proponents of Baal (I Kings 19:14).[2]

The epoch which Elijah shared with Ahab and Jezebel, the second quarter of the ninth century, had its prophets, so designated, in profusion, adherents both of Baal and Yahweh (I Kings 18; 20; 22), and in professional group association both with sanctuary and court. The term "prophet," we think, referred to these in its common and primary connotation and was, therefore, only later applied to Elijah in an age when the definition of the word had been broadened to include the singular, classical prophet.

In the case of two other ninth century prophets, Micaiah (I Kings 22) and Elisha (II Kings 2-9; 13), there is no reason to doubt that they were so designated by their contemporaries. Both appear—if in exceptional roles—in association with group prophetism; Micaiah with Ahab's official court prophets and Elisha with the cult-related "sons of the prophets" at Bethel (II Kings 2:3), Jericho (II Kings 2:5), and Gilgal (II Kings 4:38; cf. 6:1). These "sons of the prophets" (first appearing in Elijah's day in I Kings 20:35) are in direct descent from the "bands of prophets" encountered more than a century earlier in the Saul narratives (I Sam. 10:5, 10) and are no doubt closely related to varied forms of the practice of group prophetism occurring without interruption between.

Samuel was Samuel or the Seer; Ahijah was probably simply Ahijah or the Shilonite, and Elijah was Elijah or the Tishbite. Prophets in truth they were, as seen from the later vantage point of the matured form of classical prophetism. But they were hardly commonly identified as "prophets" in their own day. Nathan, Micaiah, and Elisha on the other hand—certainly also prophets in the later sense—were contemporaneously known as prophets, since to be a prophet was to exist in professional association and relationship.

It is only so that the categorical protest of Amos can be understood. Amos in the middle of the eighth century reflects the common definition of "prophet" as denoting professional association, down to this time deemed necessarily neither bad nor good. Group prophetism has thus far been both of Yahweh and Baal; and as of Yahweh, neutral as associated with Saul, "good" as associated with Obadiah (I Kings 18:13; cf. 19:14) and Elisha, and on the whole, "bad" as contrasted with one of their own number Micaiah, in relationship to Ahab's court (I Kings 22). "Amaziah said to Amos, 'O seer, go, flee away to the land of Judah, and eat bread there, and prophesy there; but never again prophesy at Bethel. . . .' Then Amos answered Amaziah 'I am no prophet, nor a prophet's son.'" (Amos 7:14.) More precisely, the last line reads, "I am not a prophet, and I am not a son of a prophet." It is of course possible to translate "was" rather than "am." Grammatically it may even be equally possible, as some have insisted.[3] Contextually, however, it does not appear to be at all natural, despite efforts to make it appear so. Amos denies, not necessarily in heat, and certainly not in necessary repudiation of the institution of prophetism, that he represents what Amaziah has just imputed to him. He has had no contact with the professional, associated prophets: "Yahweh took me from following the flock, and a Yahweh said to me, 'Go, prophesy to my people Israel'" (Amos 7:15). His action here at Bethel is inspired out of this personal confrontation with Yahweh, not in any group stimulation. Not that institutional prophetism may not and does not have this valid, authentic function, nor that Amos is unwilling to be cast in a prophetic role (Amos 3:3-8 indicates the contrary!) —but simply that the group phenomenon happens not to be his origin, as charged by Amaziah.

One suspects that a change in the content of the term "prophet" occurs, in fact, with Amos and that men of prophetic temperament and function but without professional affiliation who preceded Amos came to be called "prophet" only after him. With Amos, and no doubt in retrospective regard of earlier prophets similarly confronted by the "Word of Yahweh," the term and office of prophet was expanded to include him who without benefit of group stimulation heard the Word of Yahweh and who, knowing that the Lord Yahweh had spoken, could but prophesy:

The lion has roared: who will not fear?
The Lord Yahweh has spoken: who can but prophesy? (Amos 3:8.)

Their Relationship to King and Word

These remarkable prophetic figures from the tenth and ninth centuries inform us of the emergent form of classical prophetism. Although they differ radically from one another and appear in widely varied contexts, in two regards these early prophets testify to a prophetic continuum from pre-monarchic times (and even from the age of Moses) to the decay and collapse of monarchy in Israel and on into the days of Jewish reconstruction. These prophets from Samuel to Elisha are fully prophetic first in their address to history, their passionate conviction that Yahweh's existence impinges with radical effect upon the political institution. Samuel, Nathan, Ahijah, Elijah, Micaiah, and Elisha—all, without exception—are intimately concerned with the life of the state, are crucially involved in the most decisive crises of the nation's history, and come into abrupt, psychologically violent contact with the king—that symbol in Israel embracing the absolute totality of the being of a people.[4]

74

This is the first regard. The second consistently prophetic quality appearing in this pre-Amos succession of prophets and setting them decisively apart from the prevailing institution-alized forms of prophetism is their relationship and respon-sibility to the *debar Yahweh*, the Word of Yahweh, their re-sponse to it, and their proclamation of it. In all these (it is weakest, to be sure, in Elisha) the address to history takes its content from the Word and the divine impingement upon history is made articulate and interpreted by that same Word. The Word may not yet be consciously defined as the entity, the effective, effecting, efficacious singularity which it is lyrically proclaimed to be in the sixth century:

> For as the rain and the snow
> come down from heaven,
> And return not thither
> but water the earth,
> Making it bring forth and sprout
> Giving seed to the sower
> and bread to the eater,
> So shall my word be
> that goes forth from my mouth;
> It shall not return to me empty,
> But it shall accomplish
> that which I purpose,
> And prosper in the thing for which I sent it.
> (Isa. 55:10 ff.)

At the same time, however, one must insist that this later definition of the Word is possible only as the result of an extended period during which the Word was essentially, if increasingly, so understood.

75

The first use of the phrase *debar Yahweh,* the Word of Yahweh, as an effecting instrumental entity appears in Gen. 15:1, 4, where, in all probability, the E material is first employed.[5] This same concept of the *debar Yahweh* is more sharply expressed in the Balaam oracle of Num. 23:19 ff. (in present form also from the E material) :

> God is not man, that he should lie,
> Or a son of man, that he should repent.
> Has he said, and will he not do it?
> Or has he spoken, and will he not fulfil it? (23:19.)

The sense of the divine word as accomplishing its own content is further emphasized in the next verse, when Balaam declares:

> Behold I received a command to bless:
> He has blessed, and I cannot revoke it. (23:20.) [6]

There is reason to think that both these passages reflect Israelite prophetism no later than the ninth century,[7] and it is not impossible that the Balaam oracle rests upon a much earlier original form. In any case, there can be no question of the central function of the Word in the succession of prophets beginning with Samuel and Nathan.

Samuel appears in the narratives which bridge the epoch of the judges and the time of the established monarchy. The present literary structure in Samuel appears to be the result of combining multiple and, at points, radically differing strata of tradition.[8] Despite striking ambiguities in the portrayal of Samuel, however, the stories about him present in two crucial regards a unified impression: He played the most instrumental single role in the ascendancy and demise of Saul as first king in Israel, and he, more than any other man, is responsible for the inauguration of David and the Davidic dynasty. When later tradition interprets Moses as a performing prophet, as a prophet whose primary medium is not utterance, but action, we wonder if this may not reflect typological characterization at least in part; the tendency, that is, to see in Moses and Samuel a common "type," playing similarly vigorous, creative historical roles. In any case, even when allowances are made for heightening and expansion inherent in the nature of the tradition, even admitting that a purely "photographic" image is ultimately irrecoverable, Samuel and Moses are in a unique class as performers on behalf of Yahweh. Their extreme output of work and energy is awesome. One is instrumental in the creation of a people, a nation; the other in the establishment of a political state.

As in the case of Moses, Samuel's revolutionary historical performance is recorded for its "isness," because of the living effects of Samuel's existence in the continuing present. No doubt earlier and later strata of tradition are now combined in the single account. No doubt one of tradition's opinions assessed the monarchy as in divine intent beneficent, another as negative divine judgment already taking effect. It is unmistakable that this conflict in interpretation has been imposed upon the present portrayal of Samuel. Nor is there any doubt that the image of a prophetic form emergent in the century or two following Samuel has inevitably been retrojected upon Samuel in the course of a continuingly fluid process of transmission (this is especially conspicuous in I Sam. 1-3; 7). Nevertheless, while the image is in no sense photographic, while any actual and precise "vital statistics" may be irredeemable, a portrait remains. The artist, tradition, has quite properly been involved in the creation of an image, exercising an appropriate interpretive function, but tradition has produced the portrait working originally from a life model, from a living presence.

It would be wrong, then, to say that tradition reads back into the person of Samuel a relationship to the "Word of Yahweh" which appears only much later in the history of prophetism. In the case of Samuel, tradition employs a more refined and deeply connotative language to describe the phenomenon—a language which is a product of later and more sensitively developed prophetism. But there is no reason to doubt that the essential relationship of prophet and Word existed in Samuel. Samuel was Samuel because of the Word.

Nor is there any reason to doubt that the interpretive artistry of tradition has at certain areas in the portrait coincided with what would be the photograph, as, for example, when Samuel says to Saul: "Tell the servant to pass on before us, and when he has passed on stop here yourself for a while, that I may make known to you the Word of God [*debar 'elohim,* not *Yahweh*]." (I Sam. 9:27.) Further, tradition's interpretation is sound, and the portrait is essentially true when it ascribes to Samuel that which in essence if not in form, in content if not in exact vocabulary, could have come directly to the prophet only through the medium of the Word:

78

> Has Yahweh as great delight in burnt offerings . . .
> As in obeying the voice of Yahweh?
> Behold to obey is better than sacrifice
> And to hearken than the fat of rams. (I Sam. 15:22.)

These words are thrown at Israel's first king, Saul, who becomes King Saul at the instigation of the same Word through the same prophet. The prophet continues, prophet to king, defining another decisive turning point of history:

> Because you have rejected the word of Yahweh
> He has also rejected you from being king! (I Sam. 15:23.)

We may have doubts of the precise vocabulary. We may question the use of this stylized phrase "the Word of Yahweh" with this specific, implicit content before, at the earliest, the time of Elijah. But we do not doubt the functioning of the Word in the life and time of Samuel and his essential awareness of its entity and nature. In Samuel the effective juxtaposition of the life of Yahweh upon the course of history begins to come to human consciousness, begins to achieve articulation, in the form of the Word of Yahweh to the prophet.

Nathan appears in Samuel and Kings only in three scenes, but each time in immediate relationship to King David. In II Sam. 7 he responds to the king's expressed desire to build an appropriate "house" for the ark of God.[9] In II Sam. 12 he confronts David with the king's heinous performance in the Bathsheba affair and pronounces Yahweh's judgement on king and kingdom. Finally, Nathan appears in that crowded

79

scene of David's last recorded official day, I Kings 1, to play a decisive role in Solomon's accession.

In the present form of the narrative the Word of Yahweh is prominently featured in the first two scenes, where it bears, as in the case of the Samuel stories, the sense of a definition only later fully crystallized. The Word is equally crucial in the third scene by its very absence. In the first scene the word countermands the first affirmative response of Nathan to David (II Sam. 7:4 ff.). In the second it is entirely at the inspiration and direction of the Word that the prophet devastatingly confronts and convicts the king, and it is the content of the Word which he then pronounces in judgment ("Thus says Yahweh!" [II Sam. 12:7, 11]). Where the Word is so indispensably cast in the first two scenes, it can be no accident of the text that there is not even a suggestion of Nathan's acting as the instrument of the Word in the third scene. As in the opening of the first scene (II Sam. 7:1-3), the recorders of the drama visualize Nathan acting on his own. In I Kings 1-2 (a continuation of that incomparable narrative of II Sam. 9-20) the failure to affirm Solomon's accession by the Word must constitute at least an editorial indictment of Solomon and the conspiracy which made him king. The intentional silence with reference to the Word testifies further to the sharpening sense of the entity of the Word in the tenth century.[10]

Still in the tenth century, it is king and Word brought into radically effective concord through the prophetic function of Ahijah the Shilonite (I Kings 11:29 ff.; 12:15). Another particularly decisive and consequential event in Israel's history, the secession of the northern tribes and the establishment of two political states in the place of one, is instigated by the word through the prophet Ahijah to the king-to-be Jeroboam I.

About a century later another king-to-be, this time Jehu, is confronted by the Word (II Kings 9:6). Elisha and his "young man, the prophet" act upon and pronounce what is represented as the Word with, again, radically effective results. In view of Jehu's subsequent reprehensible behavior and classical prophetism's ultimate repudiation of any true relationship between Jehu and the Word (Hosea 1:4), we should judge either that this word was not the Word; or that Jehu viciously appropriated the divine Word in Elisha to his own brutal ambitions. The first alternative is perhaps editorially entertained. Elisha is, like Nathan in II Sam. 7:1-3, represented as acting on his own in dispatching one of the prophets to Jehu (II Kings 9:1).

The imposition of Word upon king is sharply attested again in that brilliant scene immediately preceding the death of Ahab in the middle of the ninth century (I Kings 22). The Word through Micaiah works its radical historical effects, and another prophet is instrumental in the efficacious juxtaposition of divine life and will upon human events.

King and Word are brought into most moving conflict in the collision of Ahab and Elijah earlier in the second quarter of the ninth century. The Word to David through Nathan involved the dual indictment for adultery and murder; to Ahab through Elijah it indicts for murder and theft—"Have you killed and also taken possession!" (I Kings 21:19.) In Elijah, however, the Word becomes more consciously an instrumental entity, and for the first time (in the narratives

81

of I Kings 17-19; 21) we suspect a contemporaneous apprehension by a prophet of the Word that is substantially the Word of classical prophetism.

Note first the relative frequency and consistency of the term "the Word" (of Yahweh) in the Elijah narratives: I Kings 17:2, 5, 8, 16, 24; 18:1 (31, 36 secondary?) ; 19:9 21:17 (28 secondary?) .[11] Note also that, as in the usage of later classical prophetism, the Word here conveys the sense of a formula, a known formula, the content, nature, and potency of which are widely familiar now. Note further that the Word is associated not only with the king but with the people as well. It creates (I Kings 17) and terminates (I Kings 18) the drought, a judgment upon people as well as king. It is surely instrumental in the prophet's indictment of the Carmel assembly (I Kings 18:20 ff.) , "How long will you go limping with two different opinions?" (Cf. Elijah's lament in 19:14 that the people of Israel have forsaken Yahweh.) It is, of course, the Word which sends the prophet back from Horeb (I Kings 19:15 ff.) , not in the role of palace prophet to the king and queen, but to minister again to the nation, in the good company of multitudes still faithful to Yahweh.[12]

In the manner of the Word to Samuel (I Sam. 15) and to Nathan (II Sam. 12) , the instrumental Word is applied through Elijah in judgment of the king (I Kings 21:17 ff) . Elijah belongs to the company of preclassical prophets from Samuel to Elisha. At the same time, however, and more than any other in the company, he anticipates in two regards that succession of prophets beginning with Amos to which he is in a peculiar way the forerunner. Elijah alone of all prophets properly belongs to both groups. In Elijah the Word has attained substantially full prophetic definition and form. Through him the Word finds its mature prophetic expression and application, not merely, or even principally, to the king, but to the nation, the whole people of the covenant. Yahweh's Word impinges now decisively upon the history of Israel with such force as implicitly to involve all history or upon the royal house with such intensity as to judge all men. Jesus condenses the Old Testament prophetic ethic (quoting from Deuteronomy and Leviticus) when he declares that "all the law and the prophets" depend upon love of God and love of neighbor (Matt. 22:35-40; cf. Mark 12:28-31). In reality, however, he reaches ultimately back to Elijah, in whom for the first time in biblical record these two propositions find impassioned expression in a single life. The divine life confronts, is involved in, and decisively qualifies the life of history. To repudiate it ("the people of Israel have forsaken thee"), to delimit it or run in the face of it ("Have you killed and also taken possession?"), to attempt to compromise with it ("How long will you go limping with two different opinions?") is not mere folly, but unqualified disaster resulting at best in the loss of meaning and fulfilment and at worst in the imposition of chaos and death. In the passionate intensity of Elijah all men and all history are implicitly embraced. It remains the task and function of classical prophetism to make concrete and specific the decisive involvement of Yahweh in historical existence.

NOTES

[1] This, and related problems of I Kings 17-19; 21; II Kings 1-2, are discussed in detail in my unpublished doctoral dissertation, *The Historical Problem of Elijah,* in the Yale University Library.

[2] The statement in the commission to Elijah that "Elisha . . . you shall anoint to be prophet in your place" (I Kings 19:16) is itself, together with its context, saturated with problems. In my judgment (and that of some other commentators) the Commission (I Kings 19:15b-17 [but retaining vss. 15a and 18]) was no part of the original Elijah texts.

[3] Rowley, *The Servant of the Lord,* p. 114, n. 2.

[4] See Johnson, *Sacral Kingship in Ancient Israel,* pp. 2 ff., and all footnotes thereto appended. As Johnson puts it, "the nation as a psychical whole [has] its focus in the royal house and, at any given time, in the reigning monarch." See also J. Pedersen, *Israel* (London and Copenhagen, 1940), III-IV, 81 ff.

[5] Von Rad, *Genesis,* pp. 176 ff. (German: pp. 152 ff.).

[6] That is, unless one prefers the Septuagint reading in 23:20b, which has Balaam, not Yahweh, as subject:

> Behold, I received a command to bless
> *I* will bless and I will not reverse it.

See *The Interpreter's Bible,* 2, 257.

[7] A. Weiser, *The Old Testament: Its Formation and Development,* translated by Dorothea M. Barton (*Einleitung in das Alte Testament* [Göttingen, 1949]) (New York: Association Press, 1961), pp. 124 ff. (German: pp. 97 ff.), would date these texts after Elijah (that is, *ca.* 850) but sometime before Jeroboam II, who came to the throne in 787 or 786.

[8] *The Interpreter's Bible,* 2, 855 ff.

[9] Cf. I Chr. 17. This is the only one of the three scenes which is reproduced by the Chronicler. See also the Chronicler's reference to "the book of Nathan" in I Chr. 29:29 and II Chr. 9:29.

[10] II Sam. 9-20 plus I Kings 1-2 can hardly be later than the tenth cen-

tury. See any standard Introduction to the Old Testament. Weiser, *The Old Testament: Its Formation and Development,* pp. 65 ff. (German: p. 56), dates this remarkable work in the tenth, and includes the nucleus of II Sam. 7. as integral to it.

[11] The notice of the coming of the Word in 19:9 is premature, copied from 19:13 where, however, we should certainly read not "there came a voice to him, and said" but, as in 19:9, "the Word of Yahweh came to him and said. . . ." "Voice" in 19:13 comes into the present text under the influence of the same word at the end of vs. 12, where, however, it means "sound" rather than "voice." See the commentaries.

[12] Against the view of some who see in the 7,000 faithful who remain in Israel (I Kings 19:18) an early insinuation of the "remnant" idea.

V

The Faith of Classical Prophetism

IN THAT SUCCESSION OF PROPHETS BEGINNING ABOUT A CENTURY after Elijah there is that which is distinctly new. There is the new that is external, the emergence out of pragmatic history, out of the actual course of real events, of that which earlier was not, and could not have beeen anticipated. This is the new of the new page in history, the new of the new epoch—created out of the old, surely, but materializing as one of an inconceivably broad range of inconceivable possibilities. In Israel in the eight century it was a new charged with tragedy.

There is of course also the internal new, but it is inseparable from the external. Israel's historical existence, which was first brought into being out of Egypt, is seen in classical prophetism to be turning back again into that same essential abyss, that same chaos, that same unendurable meaninglessness. For those of the prophetic disposition from Moses to Elijah and Elisha, Egypt lay only behind. Until the middle of the eighth century Israel's future, while uncertain and often highly insecure, could be seen as in continuum with the present, as holding in prospect essentially more of the same. Now, for that same prophetic intuition "Egypt" was both before and behind. Out of an Egyptian existence formless and void Yahweh had created for Israel a life relatively

86

formed and ordered. Now, in the mind of classical prophetism Israel was destined to "return to the land of Egypt" (Hosea 11:5) as Yahweh's judgment for her failure to fulfill herself as the covenant people.

The new, both of the external history and the related internal prophetic mind of classical prophetism, was initially produced, beginning in the middle of the eighth century, simply by the aggressive ambition of Assyria, backed, for the first time in several centuries, with leadership and power to implement it.[1] Tiglath-pileser III assumed the throne of Assyria in 745 B.C., the first of an uninterrupted series of great soldiers on the throne of Assyria. He and his immediate successors quickly brought the Neo-Assyrian Empire to the peak of its power and created a political-military institution which for the first time united almost the whole of the ancient Orient under Assyrian rule.[2] Indeed, within a single decade of the accession of Tiglath-pileser all the oriental world was clearly his, either in fact or potential. By 721, when the Northern Kingdom of Israel fell to Assyria, any hopes of political existence independent of Assyria were simply fatuous. From Tiglath-pileser's days (745-27) through the successive reigns of Shalmaneser V (727-22), Sargon II (to 705), Sennacherib (to 691), and Esarhaddon (to 669), Assyria's position of world domination was beyond serious challenge. The succeeding reign of Ashurbanipal (669-32) —unlike his predecessors, a patron, not of the art of war, but of literature—was the beginning of the undoing of Assyrian world rule. Assyria succumbed to the vicious powers of the Chaldeans out of Babylon, the Medes out of the mountains of Iran, and the bands of Umman-manda (apparently Scythians) from the steppes of Russia. The long death agony of Assyria was finally ended in decisive battles of 612 and 610 B.C. This provided, however, at best only a brief respite, not any fundamental departure, from surviving Israel's (Judah's) untenable position. Assyria's position in the world was simply appropriated by Neo-Babylonian power. The political center of the ancient Middle East was moved from Nineveh to Babylon. The sentence of political death was imposed upon Judah by Nebuchadnezzar in the first two decades of the sixth century. The cycle was complete. Israel once more became without form and void. She was once more swallowed up in the chaos of captivity. From uncreation to creation, she was now relegated again to the uncreated: Out of Egypt, into this land, back into Egypt.

Classical prophetism rises, then, first in the consciousness that Israel now stands between Egypts, that what she was she will be again. Heretofore in Israelite Yahwism the meaning of the present was taken primarily from the understanding and interpretation of the past, as, for example, in the ancient cultic confession of faith recorded in Deut. 6:20 ff. and employed precisely to answer the question of the meaning (so vs. 20) of the present: "We were Pharaoh's slaves in Egypt; and the Lord brought us out of Egypt with a mighty hand . . . that he might bring us in and give us the land which he swore to give to our fathers." (6:21, 23.) Israel's present relatively ordered existence is the creation of God out of former disorder and is to be understood and accepted as his creative gift in fulfillment of his free promise to the patriarchs. The confession addresses the future, if at all, only implicitly. In quality the future is of a piece with the present: "now" embraces tomorrow and tomorrow[3]—in all of which, appropriate response to the confessional knowledge of meaning in history is faithful participation in the Yahweh cultus. Such is the sense of Deut. 6:24 (cf. 26:10, the interpretative conclusion of a comparable cultic confession in 26:5-9) : "And the Lord commanded us to do all these statutes, to fear the Lord our God, for our good always, that he might preserve us alive, *as at this day."*

Preclassical Yahwism understands the past and present chiefly in terms of Yahweh's *positive* action on behalf of Israel. If the future is addressed at all, it is with the confident expectation that it will be in predictable conformity with the past. The prophets from Amos on are forced to reinterpret the meaning of the present in terms of an immediate future to be charged with tragedy—but a tragedy no less the result of divine action than the great formative event of redemption from Egypt. For the classical prophet the two-member scheme, "out of Egypt, into this land," has become the three-member scheme, "out of Egypt, into this land, into Egypt again."

Yahweh, who redeemed the nation for his own purposes will now *for the same essential purposes* commit the nation to its preredeemed status of chaos and meaninglessness. Why? What lies beyond the second Egypt? Is there a fourth and final member to be added to the three-member scheme? What does all this mean? How does this qualify the nature of existence under God in the very present time? These were questions consciously and unconsciously addressed by the classical prophets, questions the answers to which are conditioned and shaped by the great prophets' understanding of a number of concepts, notably, Word and symbol, election and covenant, rebellion, judgment, compassion, redemption, and finally, consummation. Five of these concepts appear in integrated form in the eleventh chapter of Hosea. Whether or not this is from the prophet Hosea, it is a fully characteristic expression of the mind and faith of classical prophetism. The first of these concepts, Word and symbol, is everywhere prominent in the prophetic canon. The seventh and last appears most prominently in the collection of prophetic utterances now under the name of Isaiah, and especially in the block of chapters conventionally assigned to the so-called Second Isaiah, chs. 40-55.

"Thus Says Yahweh": Word and Symbol

We have already discussed the nature and significance of the Word of Yahweh in its role in pre-Amos prophetism. The concept obviously underlying the use of the Word in the Elijah narratives makes clear that certainly by the eighth century the prophetic understanding of the Word was matured and substantially established. As we have seen, it was regarded as an entity containing and releasing divine power to accomplish itself—that is, to perform or bring to pass its content. The Word of Yahweh was, emphatically, a dynamic Word.

In the classical prophets it appears in a new relationship with the prophet himself and the prophet's call, his sense of vocational commitment. To a greater or lesser degree in all the great classical prophets one sees the phenomenon of the psychology of captivity, a self-consciousness in vocation characterized by feelings of having been overpowered by the Word of Yahweh.

> The lion has roared;
> who will not fear?
> The Lord Yahweh has spoken;
> who can but prophesy? (Amos 3:8.)

Here is the same instrumental Word, exercising the power of seizure over the same prophet: "The Lord *took* me from following the flock, and the Lord *said* to me, 'Go, prophesy to my people Israel.' " (Amos 7:15.)

The role of the Word of Yahweh is essentially the same in the remarkable call narratives of Isaiah (ch. 6), Jeremiah (ch. 1), and Ezekiel (chs. 1 ff.), but the sense of professional bondage to the Word is everywhere apparent in the prophetic canon and appears most eloquently and movingly in the so-called Confessions of Jeremiah—not always explicitly, to be sure, but quite unmistakably. In one of the most intense of these outbursts, the sharp entity of the Word of Yahweh and its commanding power over the prophet are thus expressed:

> The Word of Yahweh has become for me
> a reproach and derision all day long.
> If I say, "I will not mention him,
> or speak any more in his name,"
> there is in my heart as it were
> a burning fire shut up in my bones,
> and I am weary with holding it in,
> and I cannot! (20:8b-9.)

The prophetic sense of the entity and power of the Word explains in great part the concentrated emotional character

91

of the prophets and their sometimes deep anguish in proclaiming the negative message, the pronouncement of doom
upon the life of the political state. If the prophets suffer in
their role it is not merely the result of a natural distaste for
uttering what is unpleasant to their hearers. Rather, the
prophetic anguish is the product of the prophet's inevitable
sense of participation in and, consequently, responsibility
for the negative Word. To speak in the name of Yaweh and
under the formula "Thus says Yahweh!" of approaching
catastrophe is, in the prophetic psychology, to take a positive hand in the destructive event—to release, in the very
proclamation of doom, the power to produce the debacle.
This negative Word may and often does carry within itself
the quality of contingency. Destruction is predicated on the
present faithless and rebellious structure of the total life of
the covenant people. The word of destruction may be can-
celled by repentance, a possibility which renders the prophetic proclamation only the more intense, desperate, and
anguished.

What is true of the Word is also true of the symbolic acts
of the prophet. Hosea's and Isaiah's symbolic naming of their
children, for example (Hos. 1; Isa. 7 and 8) and the singular
and sometimes weird dramatizations of Jeremiah, and even
more Ezekiel, are graphic extensions of the Word, possessing
both for the prophet and his observer-hearer a quality of
realism psychologically unfathomable to the Western mind.
When the prophet speaks that which he represents to be the
Word of God it is to him emphatically the Word of God.
The prophets' use of the phrase is no courteous condescen-
sion to conventional piety, no variety of innocent lie

thoroughly stylized to mean in fact the word of man. In the prophetic psyche this Word is initiated by God. It is impellingly dynamic. It breaks through human life, human time, and into human history, and in doing so, it possesses and releases its own power, with or without the consent of the human instrument through whom the Word is proclaimed. Observe in the Old Testament that even the word of a man, solemnly spoken under certain more or less formalized circumstances, for example, in curse or blessing, cannot be retracted or set aside. Once spoken, the power inhering even in the human word is released beyond recall.[4] How much more so with the Word of Yahweh in the mouth of the prophet!

The symbolic act of the prophet was regarded in ancient Israel, and especially in the prophets' own understanding, as, then, an even more intense and efficacious phenomenon than the spoken Word. These sometimes strange and always dramatic actions of the prophets charged with dire symbolic meaning are never *merely* symbols. The dramatized Word even more than the uttered Word is deemed to be charged with the power of performance.

Now if, in addition to all of this, we recall another psychological phenomenon in ancient Israel, the normative sense of corporate personality among the people of Israel (and the East in general, as over against the West), we are in a position to understand as fully as is possible the personality of Jeremiah or Ezekiel. In Word and symbol they become, in a sense, executioners acting at the command, with the authority, and under the power of Yahweh. But in their sense of corporate personality, their understanding of community life in terms of the one identified with the many and the many caught up and embodied in the one, these prophets become in effect their own executioners. In the destructive Word and symbol directed at the people they are themselves, in profoundly realistic psychological meaning, destroyed!

From this sense none of the great classical prophets is totally free. Amos is misinterpreted as an "objectifier" of the nation, phychologically extricating himself therefrom. Ezekiel is often charged with the successful suppression of any instincts of a participating, identifying compassion. That Ezekiel appears in pronounced contrast to Jeremiah in this respect is certain. But I think we rightly understand Ezekiel only when we recognize that the intensity and frequency of his destructive symbolisms must have made a self-induced callousness imperative. Not that Ezekiel succeeded in this endeavor with consistency, as witness, for example, 9:8; 11: 13; 36:25-32.

The prophetic use of the efficacious Word and symbol is probably an item of survival out of primitive magic. Much in the Old Testament is derived from the pagan, the crude, the superstitious, to be refined and re-created in the Yahweh faith of Israel. If the prophetic use of symbol represents a survival of sympathetic—that is, mimetic—magic the transformation is striking. Magic is coercive of the unseen powers. The prophet is overwhelmed by the sense of Yahweh's coerciveness, and the prophetic symbol, so far from aiming at control of the deity, is inspired, performed, and interpreted at the behest of the Word of Yahweh to bring to pass the judgment and will of Yahweh in Israel and the world.

"Out of Egypt I Called My Son": Election and Covenant
(Hos. 11:1)

The notion of Israel as a chosen people elected by Yahweh for special reasons and for a particular purpose is by no means peculiar to the classical prophets. Election is primarily expressed by the verb *baher, bḥr,* to choose. It is the sense of the term that one object is freely chosen from among multiple possibilities. The idea of election is also positively conveyed in varying qualities in terms of the call, *qrʾ,* of belonging, *qnh,* of separation, *hibdil,* of setting apart, *hiqdish,* and of knowing, *ydʿ.*[5]

The actual term for covenant, *berit,* appears rarely if at all in the classical, pre-exilic prophets. The few occurrences of the term have been regarded as unauthentic by most literary critics. The proposal that the term itself is essentially of postexilic origin in Israel is hardly tenable. It may be that the word "covenant" was deliberately avoided by the great prophets because it was popularly misunderstood and misappropriated. Covenant no doubt often represented Israel's superiority and so became the very basis of a narrow, prideful, exclusive nationalism. But though the term is rare or even non-existent in the classical prophets, the sense of covenant is unmistakably present—covenant as the working extension and implementation of election, the formal application of what is implicit in election, namely, the concrete responsibilities assumed by the Elector and the obligations of the electee freely undertaken in response.

Election is perpetuated and realized in covenant.[6] Covenant in the Old Testament is the working contract between unequal parties, initiated by the senior partner in the act of election. The two concepts must be seen together.

This condition of having been chosen and of continuing to exist in a state of chosenness is expressed by the prophets in a variety of analogies. The relationship of Yahweh to Israel is expressed in the father/son image (for example, in addition to Hos. 11, Isa. 1:2), owner/vineyard (Isa. 5; 27), shepherd/flock (especially Isa. 40:11), potter/clay (so Jer. 18; see also Isa. 29:16; 64:8: Heb. vs. 7), and of course predominantly, husband/wife (Hosea, as the fundamental thesis; Jer. 2:1-7; 3:11-22; Ezek. chs. 16 and 23; Isa. 50:1; 54:5; 62:4-5).[7]

In classical prophetism the interpretation of Israel's existence is everywhere dependent upon the concept of election/covenant. The meaning of Israel's historical life, past, present, and future, is prophetically apprehended and proclaimed upon what is deemed to be this absolutely fundamental reality. If the prophets speak, as they do, with fierce eloquence on behalf of justice and righteousness in the social and economic life of their people, they are preaching no general, abstract morality, no goodness-for-goodness'-sake ideology, but specifically and pointedly an election/covenant ethic. The sense of the prophetic ethic and morality is always something like this: "You shall refrain from this practice, or you shall do thus-and-so, because I am Yahweh who brought you up out of Egypt [election] and you are a people voluntarily committed in return to the performance of my just and righteous will [covenant]." The motivation of the prophetic ethic is election. The nature of that ethic is determined by the covenant.

So it is, emphatically, in what now follows under the headings rebellion, judgment, compassion, redemption, consummation. As the prophet addresses himself with intense concentration to his own generation in his own land he indicts his people on behalf of the deity (for their rebellion), proclaims God's negative response (judgment), identifies his own and God's anguish and effects its resolution with the declaration of the love of God for Israel (compassion), moves to the proclamation of the nation's fulfillment (redemption), and finally beyond that to her completion of universal mission (consummation). All this he does in the immutable context of election/covenant.

"They Went from Me": Rebellion
(Hos. 11:2)

It is important to observe that the prophetic castigation embraces, if apparently sometimes incidentally, not simply Israelite man, but man. One thinks in this connection, not only of direct indictment in prophetic discourse (for example, Isa. 10:5 ff. and Amos 1-2), but also of the collection and arrangement of oracles against foreign nations going on in prophetic circles and resulting in such blocks of material in the prophetic canon as Isa. 13-23; Jer. 46-51; Ezek. 25-32. In the prophetic faith, if not always in specific articulation, all men and all nations are in rebellion against God, denying in multiple ways the appropriate terms of human existence under the active rule of the righteous Yahweh.

For the prophet, however, Israel stands immovable, inextricable, at the very hub of human existence and as the precise nucleus of the vast area of God's concern. She is the electee of God, the covenanter with him. She, and in a profound sense she only, is the wife, the clay, the flock, the vineyard, or the son of God, who is in turn, and respectively, the husband, the potter, the shepherd, the landowner, or the father. Not that prophetism as a whole would exclude non-Israelites from meaningful relationship with God:

> "Are you not like the Ethiopians to me,
> O people of Israel," says the Lord.
> "Did I not bring up Israel from the land of Egypt,
> and the Philistines from Caphtor
> and the Syrians from Kir?" (Amos 9:7.)

In that day Israel will be the third with Egypt and Assyria, a blessing in the midst of the earth, whom the Lord of hosts has blessed, saying, "Blessed be Egypt my people, and Assyria the work of my hands, and Israel my heritage." (Isa. 19:24.) [8]

But the prophet does assume in the God-Israel relationship a different quality from the God-nations relationship. There is an intensity and intimacy, and ultimately a purpose and mission, uniquely present here which leads Amos, for example, to cry in the name of Yahweh:

> "You only have I known
> of all the families of the earth;
> therefore I will punish you
> for all your iniquities." (3:2.)

Israel's rebellion against God is shared by all peoples, to be sure, but her rebellion is uniquely and totally conditioned by the quality of her relationship to God and is therefore, in prophetic judgment, the more heinous.

Her rebellion against Yahweh is grossly, flagrantly displayed in the totality of her life. The whole head is sick and the whole heart faint. The alienation is willful and complete. Israel is utterly estranged. (See Isa. 1:4 ff.) The extended and most bitter indictments in the three largest prophetic collections[9] as well as the sweeping, often ferocious, denunciations in Amos, Hosea, Micah, and the later Isaiahs[10] make it clear that no distinction existed for the prophet between the rebelliousness expressed in social-economic-political malpractice on the one hand and cultic-religious-theological deviation on the other. Finally, the totality of Israel's rebelliousness is, in the prophetic understanding, the shocking betrayal of Israel's pride and arrogance, which appear all the more reprehensible against the background of such relationships as father/son, owner/vineyard, and husband /wife:

> Sons have I reared and brought up,
> but they have rebelled against me. (Isa. 1:2.)

> What more was there to do for my vineyard,
> that I have not done in it?
> Yet when I looked for it to yield grapes,
> why did it yield vile-smelling [R.S.V., wild] grapes? (Isa. 5.4.)

> I remember the devotion [hsd] of your youth,
> your love as a bride. . . .
> And I brought you into a plentiful land. . . .
> But when you came in you defiled my land,
> and made my heritage an abomination. (Jer. 2:2, 7.)

I plighted my troth to you. . . .
> But you trusted in your beauty and played the
> harlot. (Ezek. 16:8, 15.)

Israel's rebelliousness is infidelity; her infidelity, pride. And the rebellion against God that is human pride is ultimately in prophetism castigated in all men; for Israelite prophetism knows, if Israel forgets, that Israel's rotten, unholy pride, productive only of a sickness unto death, is fully shared by all men! [11]

"They Shall Return to Egypt": Judgment
(Hos. 11:5)

In Hebrew "to judge," *shpt,* and its derivatives convey considerably more than corresponding English terms. The act of judging is one in which wrong is righted, either by punishment of the aggressor, by restitution to the victim, or by both. In the Old Testament the underprivileged are to be "judged" (e.g., Isa. 1:17: "judge the fatherless, plead for the widow") as well as willful offenders. Judgment, then, is the realization of justice.

We have already observed that the sense of impending negative judgment upon Israel is a formative characteristic of classical prophetism. The prophets of the eighth to the sixth centuries are all predominantly oriented in catastrophe —either the fall of the Northern Kingdom in 721 or the end of the surviving Southern state in 587—whether they stand before or after the envisaged tragedy. Unequivocally for them this temporal-historical-political event is divine judgment, the creation and establishment of justice, the rebalancing of the scales between Yahweh and Israel. The judge, the performer of the act of judgment, is Yahweh himself. The object of the judgment is Israel. The act of judgment is political death, a figurative return to Egypt. If this is an experience seemingly of unqualified catastrophe for Israel, if it is a return to an existence formless and meaningless, it nevertheless had its own kind of order and meaning. It rights the wrong, and more, much more, it provides the now rectified context for a resumption of the relationship between Yahweh and Israel which obtained after the first Egypt and before the conditions responsible for the bitter experience of the second Egypt.

Judgment is right. It is of Yahweh. And he still rules.

The prophets, from Amos and Isaiah before the destructive events, to the subsequent Isaiahs and other prophets after the final catastrophe, proclaim the judgment with staggering power and in stunning language. They entertain personal hopes that it may be averted or that it will work for good in an Israel that loves God, but this affects not at all the uncompromised character of the negative proclamation.

> Thus says the Holy One of Israel,
> "Because you despise this word,
>   and trust (*sic*) in oppression and perverseness . . .
> This iniquity shall be to you
>   like a break in a high wall . . .
>   which is smashed so ruthlessly
> that among its fragments not a sherd is found
>   with which to take fire from the hearth,
>   or to dip water out of the cistern!" (Isa. 30:12-
>   14.) [12]

101

The character of the judgment is conditioned by the character of Israel's rebellion. The totality of the judgment is the appropriate and necessary rectifying of the nation's totally willful, arrogant rejection of Yahweh.

> Thou hast smitten them,
>   but they felt no anguish;
> thou hast consumed them,
>   but they refused to take correction.
> They have made their faces harder than rock;
>   they have refused to repent . . .
> They have spoken falsely of Yahweh,
>   and have said, "He will do nothing" . . .[13]
> Therefore says Yahweh, the God of hosts:
> "Because they have spoken this word,
> behold, I am making my words in your mouth a fire,
>   and this people wood, and the fire shall devour them. . . ."
> (Jer. 5:3, 12, 14, but see the full section vss. 1-17.)

For all their invective, the prophets are misunderstood if their proclamation of judgment against Israel is interpreted as an arbitrary or vindictive action of Yahweh. They want to make it plain (they are demonstrably often hard put to do so because of the intensity of their own feelings and emotions) that it is judgment in the full sense—justice, the setting right of the woefully wrong. They make this plain in their not uncommon joining of the issue between Yahweh and Israel in terms unmistakably drawn from current Israelite judicial practice (cf. Amos 3:1; Hos. 4:1; Isa. 1:2, 18 ff.; 3:13; Mic. 6:1 ff.). God accuses, he renders the verdict, and he is himself responsible for the execution of judgment against Israel.

In other passages (cf. Amos 1:3 ff.; Jer. 1:15 ff.; Mic. 1:2-4; Zeph. 3:8; Joel 3:2 ff., [Heb. 4:2 ff.] the judicial setting is convoked not against Israel, but against the nations. We shall reserve our discussion of judgment that is also eschatological for the final paragraphs of this chapter, under the heading consummation.

"How Can I Give You Up?": Compassion
(Hos. 11:8)

One doubts that any of the classical prophets pronounced a divine verdict of *unconditioned* doom. Amos has often been so understood. Others of the prophets have been read as proclaimers exclusively of the negative aspects of divine judgment by resort to a literary criticism which neatly attributes the prophetic word of God's compassion to secondary sources. Now, obviously, much more originated with Amos than what is brought down to us as prophetic utterance under his name in the canon; and in what we have there is reflected the unmistakable attribution to Yahweh of the prophet's own sense of compassion. In the repeated phrase "yet have you not returned unto me" Amos makes it clear that the very catastrophe which Yahweh visits upon his people is itself an expression of his love and faithfulness, since out of this negative action he seeks to bring about a reconciliation with prideful rebellious Israel. (See Amos 4:6-11.)

The mood and language of the classical prophets as a whole to say nothing of their faith, hope, and love, make emphatic their conviction that rebellion and judgment in the context of election/covenant at once call forth compassion and redemption. The Hebrew terms denoting com-

passion—noun, verb, and adjective from a root *rḥm* of uncertain original meaning—appear not uncommonly through
the prophetic books, and sometimes in conjunction with the
root denoting love, *'hb*. But the unique quality of Yahweh's
compassion is best expressed by the prophetic language in
the term *ḥesed*.

Ḥesed is necessarily subject to several different English
renderings, according to context—mercy (a relatively infre-
quent sense, although so commonly rendered in the Septuagint), kindness, devotion, faithfulness, grace. It is a term
primarily describing and qualifying relationships—man/
man and God/man. Its fundamental root sense conveys the
quality of sustaining strength, strength in duration, and it
is commonly in the Old Testament an attribute of covenant,
either God/Israel or such family "covenantal" relationships
as husband/wife or father/son. *Ḥesed* is the strength of
faithfulness which constitutes the very life of the relationship. This sense of the word is best illustrated in Hosea,
where the ghastly double rupture of marriage and covenant
is in prophetic consciousness a *fait accompli,* and where the
prophet draws an analogy between the relationship of husband and wife and that of Yahweh and his people. The
prophet now speaks for Yahweh:

> "In that day . . . I will betroth you to me forever:
> I will betroth you to me in righteousness
> and in justice and in *ḥesed* [R.S.V., steadfast love]
> and in compassion [from *rḥm:* R.S.V., mercy]
> . . . in faithfulness
> and you shall know Yahweh." (Hos. 2:16 ff., Heb. vss.
> 18 ff.)

In the prophetic use of the term (notably in Hosea, Jeremiah, and Second Isaiah) *hesed* quite escapes the confines of covenant, or perhaps it would be better to say that as a quality of covenant it is chiefly responsible for a transformation in the concept of covenant. That covenant of which *hesed* is a part becomes in the exercise of *hesed* something vastly more than that pedestrian covenant which it was in its inception. Look again at the passage just quoted and at its context. The covenant here, both the man/woman and the God/people covenant, is finished, terminated. It comes to an end with a rupture of incredible violence and proportion. But *hesed* becomes operative in this now shattered covenant to such a transforming degree that what was covenant-with-*hesed* now becomes *hesed*-with-covenant. Covenant it still is, but utterly recreated and transformed by compassion that is *hesed*.

The same essential expansion of *hesed* beyond the limits of covenant is to be seen also in Jeremiah and Second Isaiah.

> "Return, faithless Israel," says the Lord.
> "I will not look on you in anger,
>   for I am *hasid* [adjectival form of *hesed*]," says the
>   Lord;
> "I will not be angry for ever." (Jer. 3:12.)

In Hosea the divine compassion which converts the judgment and reconstitutes the covenant is expressed in Yahweh's cry:

> "How can I give you up, O Ephraim!
> How can I hand you over, O Israel!

> . . . for I am God and not man,
>   the Holy One in your midst. . . ." (11:8 ff.)

In Jeremiah it is, "For I am *ḥasid!*"—this is the quality of my judgment and my covenant! In Second Isaiah the transforming development is completed:

> "For a brief moment I forsook you,
>   but with great compassion [*rḥm*] I will gather
>   you.
> In overflowing wrath for a moment
>   I hid my face from you,
>   but with everlasting *ḥesed*
>   I will have compassion on you," says your Redeemer, Yahweh! (Isa. 54:7 ff.)

As the poetic parallelism makes clear, the character of Yahweh's compassion is the *ḥesed* character—the steady, enduring strength of fidelity, devotion, and commitment which partakes of the quality of grace precisely because it is more than the convention of covenant can appropriately command, because it is greater than the relationship which first produced it, and because it is able, in breaking out of the relationship, to recreate the very relationship in transformed dimensions. If *ḥesed* begins in the structure of covenant, it ends with covenant as its own renewed creation.

> "For the mountains may depart
>   and the hills be removed,
> But my *ḥesed* shall not depart from you,
>   and my covenant of peace shall not be removed,"

106

> says the Lord, who has compassion on you. (Isa. 54:10.)

It is unnecessary to add that compassion of this sort is inseparably related to love, that *ḥesed* compounded of grace is itself rooted and sustained in the love of God, as it is so precisely put in Jer. 31:3:

> I have loved you with an everlasting love;
> this is why I have maintained my *ḥesed* toward you.

"I Will Return Them to Their Homes": Redemption
(Hos. 11:11)

Prophetism is the total achievement of that unique movement spectacularly witnessed in concentrated power in the eighth, seventh, and sixth centuries, but developing from the time of Israel's birth as a people out of Egypt and continuing to find essential expression in the final six or seven centuries of biblical time. This prophetism found its very being in the efficacious Word of Yahweh. This prophetism comprehended and condemned Israel's (and all men's!) appallingly arrogant posturing. This prophetism was persuaded of Israel's inescapable, cataclysmic judgment. This prophetism was equally persuaded in faith of the efficacious quality of divine compassion and *ḥesed* and in the unimpedable fulfillment of the divine purpose back of Yahweh's Word and Israel's election and covenant. Such a prophetism comes inevitably to the affirmation of Israel's historical redemption, even before the historical imposition of judgment.

In doing so, prophetism reveals the magnificent, full body of its faith. It also betrays, perhaps, the always attendant measure of its unfaith, since by and large the prophets are quite unable to envisage any ultimate establishment of divine sovereignty apart from the re-created and re-substantiated historical Israel. The prophets do not of course allow this as a point of pride. That Israel remains a part of Yahweh's redemptive purpose results, not from any indispensability of Israel to Yahweh, but simply because Yahweh so wills it. This is emphatically expressed both in Ezekiel (see 36:22-25, 32) and in Second Isaiah (Isa. 48:11) in the insistent interpretation of Israel's redemption in the divine phrase, "For my own sake I do it!" Furthermore, in the full development of prophetism faith is the victor over unfaith even in this regard. In the Servant Songs of Second Isaiah, Israel herself is seen to be ultimately expendable on behalf of the cause of the knowledge and reign of God.[13]

Prophetism exploded into full, vocal, self-conscious maturity in the historical era of Israel's existence "between Egypts." In acute awareness of an impending second Egypt (see Hos. 8:13 and 11:5) prophetism added a third member to the older two-member scheme: Out of Egypt, into this land, and now, back to Egypt. This was not the end, however. Out of the mind and faith of prophetism a fourth member in the meaningful scheme of Israel's history was added, a second act of divine redemption from chaos, redemption by return again to the land, redemption by the reconstitution of the people Israel. Out of Egypt, into this land, back to Egypt, back to this land!

Not only the third negative member, but the fourth positive element of the scheme is the work of prophetism in the eighth century. The two cannot be separated. The first Isaiah was convinced of the destruction of his people, but he was also and at once persuaded of God's compassionate purpose in judgment-justice. He was persuaded of a judgment-justice never centrally punitive in intention and quality but always itself redemptive. If judgment is wrath it is purposive wrath, not vindictive wrath. Divine judgment is never an end in itself, but that dire necessity which makes redemption possible.

> I will turn my hand against you
> and will smelt away your dross . . .
> and remove all your alloy. (Isa. 1:25.)

The prophetic declaration of a surviving remnant beyond the coming catastrophe must be understood in this light.[14] If this points to Yahweh's negative action against Israel, it is also positive in its import. We recall again Israel's habitual identification of one and many, her sense of total participation as people in *all* the meaningful events of her history, past and even future, involving one Israelite, a few, or many.[15] In the faith of Israel the glorious survival and reconstitution of a remnant is Israel's glory and Israel's re-establishment.

The understanding of historical judgment as positive in divine purpose may well be already implicit in Amos (see 4:6-11 and the discussion above). But still in the eighth century, it is most warmly expounded in Hosea (see especially 2:14-23; 5:15; 11:11). It is a pervasive if often only implicit element in the utterances of Jeremiah and makes possible that stunning declaration of a new covenant with Israel "after those days" of judgment:

109

"I will put my law within them, and I will write it upon their hearts; and I will be their God, and they shall be my people. And no longer shall each man teach his neighbor and each his brother, saying 'Know the Lord,' for they shall all know me, from the least of them to the greatest," says Yahweh; "for I will forgive their iniquity, and I will remember their sin no more." (Jer. 31:33-34.)

Redemption was purposed in the very judgment. The reconstitution, rebirth, re-creation, of Israel which was inherent in the prophetic understanding of Israel's anguished demise is given singularly vivid expression in Ezekiel's vision of the valley of death, Israel's vast open grave exposing the bare skeletons of the house of Israel. In this scene of dry death, Yahweh commands the prophet, "Prophesy [i.e., speak as prophet, speak prophetically, from the root *nb'*] . . . and say . . . , O dry bones, hear the Word of Yahweh!" (37:4).

So I prophesied as he commanded me . . . and they lived. . . . Then he said to me, "Son of man, these bones are the whole house of Israel. Behold, they say, 'Our bones are dried up, and our hope is lost; we are clean cut off.' Therefore prophesy [as above], and say to them, 'Thus says the Lord Yahweh: "Behold, I will open your graves, and raise you from your graves, O my people; and I will bring you home into the land of Israel. . . . And I will put my Spirit within you, and you shall live, and I will place you in your own land; then you shall know that I, Yahweh, have spoken, and I have done it, says Yahweh." ' " (37: 10-14.)

The form of prophetic utterance as handed down to us seldom if ever presents the single, unmitigated word of doom.

110

The much disputed positive ending of Amos, for example 9:8b ff.), may indeed be out of place, or a later addition to the text of Amos, but it is true to the structure of prophetism.

We come, now to the very eve of Israel's second historical redemption, fraught with such incredibly high hopes. The so-called Second Isaiah, believing that this second exodus signals the realization of the Word of Yahweh to the elected, covenanted Israel, speaks words moving and profound in consolation, but words which, literally taken, were only very briefly and highly approximately validated in the actual history of Israel's second redemption. (See, for example, Isa. 40:1-31; 44:21 ff.; 49:8-13.) In a lyrical, soaring projection of faith which summons the act of creation and the dramatic first exodus into the single moment of time occupied by the second exodus, the prophet cries:

> Awake, awake, put on strength,
> O arm of Yahweh;
> awake as in the days of old,
> the generations of long ago.
> Was it not thou that didst cut Rahab in pieces,
> that didst pierce the dragon? (51:9.)

This employs the old mythological language of creation and recalls the creation of the world into order and meaning by the destruction of Chaos (Rahab, the dragon).

> Was it not thou that didst dry up the sea,
> the waters of the great deep;

111

that didst make the depths of the sea a way
for the redeemed to pass over? (Vs. 10.)

In the same breath, as it were, and with the same overwhelming sense of contemporaneity, the prophet brings into the present moment of time both the creation of the world and the creation of Israel, the one by the conquest of chaos, the other by the conquest of the waters of the Red Sea. Now, with no encumbering sense of disparity in time, he couples with the acts of creation and exodus the event of Israel's second redemption which is about to take place:

> And the ransomed of the Lord shall return,
>   And come with singing to Zion;
> Everlasting joy shall be upon their heads;
>   they shall obtain joy and gladness,
>   and sorrow and sighing shall flee away. (Vs. 11.) [16]

Faith in such a measure of passion and proclaimed in such rapture cannot ultimately be contained in any concept merely of Israel's historical redemption. Prophetism produces its theology out of a process of meditation on history and the meaning of history. When its meditation is focused on what Yahweh has done in creation and exodus it is quite capable, as here, of taking wings and soaring above the plane of pedestrian history. The same prophetic theology, however, is always brought sharply back again to the realities of a frustrating historical existence. It is this tension between the alternating experiences of flight and the grim march which produces inevitably a prophetic eschatology.

A Light to the Nations: Consummation

From any point of view other than that of faith, affirmations pointing, if not beyond history, at least to a history radically transformed, are unthinkable. But if Israelite prophetism is, from our perspective, singularly nonlogical it is not nonreasonable; it adheres to its own reasonableness. If the face of existence appears to be, with only intermittent relief, as hard and as featureless as the rock, it remains an existence Yahweh-given and Yahweh-ruled. If existence appears to be obdurate, it only appears to be so, or it will be so only for a short time. All is Yahweh's, and his countenance is neither featureless nor hard: "He is gracious and merciful, slow to anger, and abounding in steadfast love" [*ḥesed*]. (Joel 2:13) [17] Moreover, Yahweh has spoken the Word that in Abraham/Israel all the nations of the earth shall be blessed (Gen. 12:3). His word cannot but accomplish that purpose to which he sends it (Isa. 55:11).

So, again we observe that the concept of *Israel's* historical redemption alone could not contain the prophetic faith or answer the questions of prophetism about the meaning of Israel's existence. Prophetism was compelled to abandon all notions—even its own—of divine purpose fulfilled in terms limited to Israel. It may even be that where the terms are of Israel's redemption, the intent (expressed in the intensity of feeling, conviction, and emotion) is universal. This is true of Isa. 51:9-11, quoted above. It is equally true of such passages—in form of Israel, in intention of all men—as Hos. 2:18-23, Jer. 23:5 ff., 29:10-14; 31:4 ff., and Isa. 9:2-7.[18] The idea of a coming Day of Yahweh as Israel's day of justification, fulfillment, and aggrandizement was violently exploded.

113

Some prophets appear to identify the Day as the actual, historical judgment/catastrophe of 722 or 587 (see Amos 5:18-20), while others make it the symbol of the final, universal judgment (see Zech. 1:14-16; Joel 2:30 ff.). Within the movement of prophetism it finally becomes that Day when Yahweh "will become king over all the earth," when "Yahweh will be one and his name one." (Zech. 14:5-9.)

Of course prophetism has its ambiguities. The structure of faith as apprehended within the whole company of the prophets was hardly without its contradictions, but the projection in faith of a final consummation embracing all prophetism's high affirmations is variously and eloquently proclaimed, and such raptured extensions of prophetic faith represent the ultimate words of prophetism.

It is appropriate now to let prophetism speak its own lines. This can best be done, I think, through the tradition of the Isaiahs. In these selected lines it is not always possible to distinguish between reality and symbol, between expectation and hope, but in prophetism's faith in consummation such distinctions are uncritical. Nor need we be concerned with the "source" of these declarations, since all come unmistakably out of Israelite prophetism.

Here is the vision of consummation to be effected through the Servant of the Lord. Nor need we be disturbed about the identity of the Servant in original prophetic understanding—whether Israel personified; the remnant of Israel; one, someone, out of Israel; or, in differing contexts, differing identities. Certainly later biblical prophets, whose works appear in the New Testament, had no hesitation in identifying Jesus Christ as the Servant.

114

And now Yahweh says,
who formed me from the womb to be his servant. . . .
"It is too light a thing that you should be my
servant to raise up the tribes of Jacob
and to restore the preserved of Israel;
I will give you as a light to the nations,
that my salvation may reach to the end of the earth." (Isa.
49:5-6.)

Whatever the form of the next passage, whatever the intentional identity of Servant and speaker, the proclamation of consummation is unambiguous, and all the more so if it is the nations who speak:

Surely he [the Servant] has borne our griefs
and carried our sorrows;
yet we esteemed him stricken,
smitten by God, and afflicted.
But he was wounded for our transgressions,
he was bruised for our iniquities;
upon him was the chastisement that made
us whole and with his stripes we are healed. (Isa.
53:4-5.)

Especially in the light of the next verse it is no wonder that Christianity sees in this Servant Song the highest projection of prophetic faith:

All we like sheep have gone astray;
we have turned every one to his own way;
And Yahweh has laid on him the iniquity of us all.
(Isa. 53:6.)

115

In Isaiah 11:1 ff. "a shoot from the stump of Jesse" will be totally endowed with the Spirit of Yahweh.

> He shall not judge by what his eyes see,
>   or decide by what his ears hear;
> but with righteousness he shall judge the poor,
>   and decide with equity for the meek of the earth.

The vision moves with tender perceptiveness to lower orders of creation among whom also the peace of righteous rule is attested with these lines in climactic description of the consummation:

> They shall not hurt nor destroy
>   in all my holy mountain;
> for the earth shall be full of the knowledge of
>   Yahweh as the waters cover the sea! (11:6 ff.)

Hear, finally, these incomparable lines referred to as the Floating Oracle because they appear both in Isaiah (2:2-4) and Micah (4:1-4):

> It shall come to pass in the latter days
>   that the mountain of the house of Yahweh
> shall be established as the highest of the mountains,
>   and shall be raised above the hills;
> and all nations shall flow to it,
>   and many peoples shall come, and say:
> "Come, let us go up to the mountain of Yahweh,
>   to the house of the God of Jacob;
> that he may teach us his ways

116

and that we may walk in his paths."
For out of Zion shall go forth the law,
    and the Word of Yahweh from Jerusalem.
He shall judge between the nations,
    and shall decide for many peoples;
And they shall beat their swords into plowshares,
    and their spears into pruning hooks;
nation shall not lift up sword against nation,
        neither shall they learn war any more. (Isa. 2:2-4.)

The book of Micah, quite possibly out of the same Isaianic circle of prophetism[19] adds a verse which contains in itself the power, the faith, and the ultimate expectation of Israelite prophetism:

They shall sit every man under his vine and under
    his fig tree.
and none shall make them afraid;
    for the mouth of Yahweh of hosts has spoken! (4:4.)

NOTES

[1] In this discussion I am particularly indebted to Von Rad, *Theologie*, I, pp. 72-76. Von Rad sees three other matters of historical change that touch intimately an understanding of the emergent form of classical prophetism. He calls attention to (1) the degeneration in syncretism of the old Yahweh faith prior to the appearance of the eighth-century prophets; (2) a kind of "emancipation" from Yahweh in increasing dependence upon the maturing structure of the political state; and (3) the dissolution of the old tribal social order with the shift of economic power to the cities, the increasing inability of the farmer, because of the burdens of heavy taxation, to maintain himself as a free man, and the growing concentration of land in the hands of a few wealthy urbanites (cf. Isa. 5:8 and Mic. 2:1 ff.) .

[2] So Martin Noth, *The History of Israel* (New York: Harper & Brothers, 1958) , p. 253.

[3] See Chap. 2, fn. 1.

[4] Cf. the Blessing of Isaac (Gen. 37) and the Oracles of Balaam (Num. 22-25) .

[5] See further Edmund Jacob, *Theology of the Old Testament* (New York: Harper & Brothers, 1958) , pp. 201 ff.

[6] But see H. H. Rowley's discussion of "Election without Covenant," *The Biblical Doctrine of Election* (London, 1950) , pp. 121 ff.

[7] Cf. Jacob, *op. cit.*

[8] Probably not from Isaiah of Jerusalem, probably relatively late, but in any case, of the very essence of classical prophetism.

[9] See especially Isa. 1:2-18; 2:6-17; 9:8-11; 29:13-16; 30:8-17; Jer. 2:4-13; 5:20-31; 7:8-11; Ezek. 16.

[10] E.g., Isa. 59:1-15.

[11] See Napier, *From Faith to Faith*, pp. 182 ff. Parts of the present discussion of prophetism appear in condensed form in my *Song of the Vineyard*, pp. 296 ff. The whole of the present study is a revision and expansion of my long article "Prophet and Prophetism" in *The Interpreter's Dictionary of the Bible* (Nashville: Abingdon Press, 1962) , pp. 896-919.

[12] See now the full chapter (Isa. 30) and compare the equally unequivocal statement of judgment in 22:14.

[13] The Hebrew here reads, literally, "He *is* not!" And as in the Babel story (Gen. 11) , this is the most horrendous apostasy—the denial, if not of his actual existence (although possibly that in Jeremiah) then of his relevance to existence. To all intents and purposes, Yahweh had as well not be.

[14] Especially in the fourth song (Isa. 52:13–53:12) .

[15] See, for example, Isaiah's symbolic naming of a son "A Remnant Shall Return" (Isa. 7:1 ff.) .

[16] Consider again, for example, the old cultic confessional phrase of Deut. 6:21, repeated generation after generation: *"We* were Pharaoh's slaves in Egypt. . . ."

[17] Cf. Von Rad, "Das theologische Problem des altestamentlichen Schöpfungsglaubens," *Werden und Wesen des Alten Testaments,* edited by J. Hempel (1936), and my article "On Creation—Faith in the Old Testament," *Interpretation,* Vol. XVI, No. 1 (January, 1962), pp. 21-42.

[18] Joel 2:13, cf. Jonah 4:2.

[19] Heb. 9:1-6. This distinction between "form" and "intention" is after C. H. Dodd, *The Kingdom of God in History,* p. 18, as quoted by R. B. Y. Scott, *The Relevance of the Prophets,* p. 153.

[20] See Chap. 2, fn. 10.

Index of Subjects

INDEX

Index of Scripture